MATTHEW SARDON

The One Way

Why Jesus Alone Leads Us to God

First published by Theosis House Press 2025

Copyright © 2025 by Matthew Sardon

All rights reserved. No part of this publication may be reproduced, stored or transmitted in any form or by any means, electronic, mechanical, photocopying, recording, scanning, or otherwise without written permission from the publisher. It is illegal to copy this book, post it to a website, or distribute it by any other means without permission.

Matthew Sardon asserts the moral right to be identified as the author of this work.

First edition

This book was professionally typeset on Reedsy. Find out more at reedsy.com

"For there is one God, and one mediator between God and men, the man Christ Jesus."
— 1 Timothy 2:5

"I am the way, and the truth, and the life; no one comes to the Father, but by me."
— John 14:6

Contents

Prologue	1
Introduction	6
1 The Human Condition: Why We Need Saving	10
2 The Old Covenant: How God Began to Reach Us	35
3 The Incarnation: When God Stepped In	62
4 The Cross: The Price of Love	91
5 The Only Mediator: One Bridge for All	119
6 Grace in the World: How Christ Reaches the Unreached	143
7 The Good Pagan and the Unknown Christ	159
8 Why Be Christian? The Joy of Knowing the Truth	181
9 The Only Door, the Open Door	206
Epilogue	221
Afterword	227
About the Author	231

Prologue

Every generation finds new words for the same old ache: *why Jesus?* Why insist that salvation hinges on one man, one moment, one cross? Why not accept that every religion is just a different accent in humanity's conversation with God?

We live in an age that prizes sincerity above truth. "It doesn't matter what you believe," people say, "as long as you're a good person." It sounds noble. It feels fair. But beneath it sits a quiet contradiction — if every belief is equally true, then truth itself has no meaning. If every road leads to the same place, then why did God bother to carve a path through history, from Abraham to Christ?

This book exists because that question refuses to die.

Not even in the modern world — perhaps least of all in the modern world — can we escape it. Every hospital ward, every warzone, every quiet grave forces us to ask: *is there a cure for death, and if so, who holds it?* Christianity claims to know. But it does not claim it out of arrogance. It claims it out of necessity.

For the Christian, the question of "why Jesus" is not about religious superiority but spiritual physics. If God is infinite and we are finite, there can only be one bridge between us — the bridge built from His side. Every other system begins with man trying to reach up; Christianity begins with God reaching down.

When Jesus said, "I am the way, the truth, and the life," He wasn't offering a slogan for exclusivists. He was describing the structure of reality. If sin has truly broken creation, then no self-improvement course, moral reform, or mystical technique can heal it. The human problem is not ignorance that needs teaching; it is separation that needs reunion. A drowning man does not need swimming lessons — he needs rescue.

That is what the Gospel announces: God has dived into the water. Every other faith tells us to climb; this one tells us that God came down the mountain. The direction is the difference.

And yet this claim offends modern sensibilities because it is so concrete. We want a God who affirms our sincerity; Christianity gives us a God who enters history. We want tolerance; He offers truth. We want advice; He offers Himself.

Still, the heart knows this story is different. Even those who deny its divinity cannot escape its gravity. No myth ever claimed that its hero was history; no philosophy ever claimed that its founder rose from the dead. Christianity dares both. It is not the story of man discovering God, but of God discovering man — over and over, until He finally steps into our world as one of us.

That's why this question persists. If Jesus really is who He said He is, then He isn't an option among many — He's the axis around which everything turns. The question "why Jesus?" is really "what is the truth about everything?"

So before we go further, let's clear the fog.

This book will not argue that Christianity is the best religion. It will show that it is the only *possible* rescue. Not because others lack goodness or wisdom, but because no other bridge can span the infinite distance between sin and holiness, life and death, creation and Creator.

This is not triumphalism; it's triage. There is one cure for what kills us, and God Himself has administered it. To say "Jesus is the only way" is not a boast — it's a diagnosis. There is only one who is both divine enough to save and human enough to represent us. Only He can repair what no one else can even reach.

The coming chapters will show how this unfolded: how God prepared the world through Israel, how He entered history through the Incarnation, how the Cross reconciled justice and mercy, and how His Resurrection made life stronger than death.

But first, we need to see *why* God would do this at all — why the Maker of galaxies would become a man, and why every other road to heaven collapses without Him.

To understand why Jesus alone is the way, we have to start with what went wrong.

The Bible's first chapters are not primitive mythology — they are spiritual realism. Humanity was created for communion with God, to share His life the way a flame shares light with the sun. Sin was not simply disobedience; it was disconnection. We cut the cord linking us to life itself, and everything that followed — pain, guilt, death — was just gravity taking effect.

That's why morality alone can't fix us. You can't legislate a corpse back to life. The problem is not that we misbehave; it's that we're separated from the Source of being. The world doesn't need a better code — it needs a cure.

Every civilization has sensed this. From the sacrifices of ancient Israel to the chants of India, from the temples of Greece to the philosophies of China, humanity has been groping for a way home. Every altar, every prayer, every moral system carries the same confession: *something's broken, and we can't mend it.* That instinct is not wrong — it's incomplete.

The human race has been trying to reach the divine with trembling hands. Christianity begins with those same hands nailed to wood — the divine reaching for us. The Gospel is not advice from a moral teacher; it's rescue from a Saviour.

When Jesus was born, God did what man could not. The infinite became finite, not to abolish human effort but to redeem it. In the

Incarnation, God ties Himself to our destiny. The chasm between holiness and sin, life and death, heaven and earth — all of it meets in one body on a cross. That's not theology; it's geometry. One vertical beam — God's descent. One horizontal beam — His embrace of the world.

That's why there can only be one Mediator. It's not intolerance; it's logic. There is only one Person who is both Creator and creature, only one who bridges the gap from both sides. Every philosopher and prophet, however noble, stands on one side of the chasm. Only Jesus stands in the middle — and by standing there, He turns the abyss into a doorway.

But here is the beauty often missed: the doorway is wide open.

The claim that Jesus is the only way is not a sentence of exclusion but a declaration of hope. If there is truly one Saviour, then salvation is possible for everyone. It no longer depends on where you were born or what language you pray in, but on whether you accept the love that has already been poured out for you.

The native who follows conscience, the child who never heard His name, the seeker who loves truth — all are reached by the same grace that flowed from the Cross. Their response may be hidden, but its source is the same Christ who descended even to the dead to call them home. Every spark of goodness anywhere in the world burns with His light, whether recognized or not.

So this book will not offer new theories; it will tell an old story made new — the only story large enough to explain the world and personal enough to save a soul. We will walk from creation to covenant, from manger to cross, from empty tomb to living Church, tracing one golden thread: God has never stopped pursuing His children.

Along the way, we'll face the hard questions modern people ask — about other religions, about good nonbelievers, about justice and mercy — and we'll see how they all lead back to the same place: the love that hung on Calvary.

    This isn't a call to win arguments. It's an invitation to come home. The world's religions may offer maps, but only one of them contains the destination. Jesus doesn't show the way; He *is* the way — because He alone has crossed from death to life and can carry us with Him.

    The claim of Christianity is not that others are lost and we are found. The claim is that everyone is lost, and One came searching. If that is true, then all history turns on a single heartbeat — the moment when the Creator took our place so we could take His hand.

    That is where the story begins.

Introduction

We live in an age that loves options. Our grocery aisles stretch endlessly with varieties of the same product. Our screens offer thousands of voices telling us what to believe, how to live, and whom to follow. Choice has become our highest creed. It should be no surprise, then, that religion has followed the same path. Spirituality today is a marketplace, not a revelation.

Across the Western world, faith has become fluid. The question "What do you believe?" is often answered with "A bit of everything." Meditation apps blend Buddhist detachment with biblical psalms. Podcasts speak of "Christ-energy" beside tarot cards and crystals. Bookshelves groan under the weight of titles promising "manifestation," "vibration," or "the universe's plan." It is called *New Age spirituality*, but it is really an old desire dressed in modern vocabulary—the ancient longing to climb back to heaven by our own means.

Alongside it grows a softer, subtler creed: *universalism*. It preaches that all religions are rivers flowing into the same sea, that sincerity matters more than truth, and that the God of Christianity differs only in name from the gods of every other faith. It feels generous and humane. It promises peace among nations and comfort to the modern conscience weary of dogma. Yet beneath its kindness lies confusion. If every path is right, none can be wrong—and truth itself becomes a matter of taste.

Even within Christianity, this language now echoes from pulpits and podcasts alike. Jesus is praised as *a* way, *a* teacher, *a* symbol of divine love among others. His uniqueness is quietly softened, His Cross reduced to metaphor, His Resurrection treated as mythic poetry. The scandal of particularity—the claim that the infinite God entered one body, one history, one crucifixion—embarrasses modern minds trained to avoid offense. The Church, fearful of seeming arrogant, sometimes forgets that humility without truth is merely surrender.

I wrote this book because the world—and the Church—needs clarity again. The claim that "all paths lead to God" sounds compassionate, but it is not true, and what is not true cannot save. If every religion could reach God, then the Incarnation was unnecessary. If enlightenment or moral improvement were enough, there would have been no Bethlehem, no Golgotha, no empty tomb. The Cross is either the center of history or the greatest misunderstanding in history. There is no middle ground.

This book is not written against those who search in other faiths. Every human heart feels the same ache: the sense that something infinite has been lost. Every act of prayer, every altar, every philosophy is humanity's attempt to recover what was broken. The purpose of this book is to show why none of those attempts, however noble, can bridge the divide—and why in Jesus Christ, God Himself has crossed it.

For centuries, thinkers have wrestled with the same question: Why must salvation come through the God-Man alone? Couldn't a merciful God forgive without such blood and agony? Couldn't He simply overlook sin and call it love? The answer is that love is precisely what cannot overlook truth. A doctor cannot heal by denying the wound. Justice and mercy are not enemies—they meet only in the Cross, where God satisfies His own justice by His own mercy. The human race could not climb to heaven, so heaven stooped down to humanity.

The uniqueness of Jesus Christ is not theological arrogance; it is metaphysical necessity. Only He unites what was separated: divinity and humanity, eternity and time. The Buddha pointed toward transcendence; Muhammad proclaimed submission; the Hindu sages sought union with the divine spark. But none of them claimed to *be* the Truth itself. Jesus does. "I am the Way, the Truth, and the Life." He does not show a road; He *is* the road. Truth, in Christianity, is not an idea but a person who can be known, loved, and crucified.

The rise of "New Age Christianity" makes this distinction urgent. Many now speak of "the Christ within" as if it were a universal energy accessible through mindfulness or moral effort. But the Christ of the Gospels is not an inner symbol—He is the incarnate Son of God who entered history, suffered under Pontius Pilate, died, and rose again. His uniqueness is not cultural; it is ontological. There is only one union of divine and human natures in a single person. There is only one empty tomb.

Universalism promises inclusion, but it quietly empties faith of content. If all claims are equally true, then none matter. The gospel of "many ways" cannot heal the world's wound because it denies there is a wound at all. The truth of Christianity is sharper: we are not lost because we lack information but because we are estranged from the Source of life. Reconciliation requires more than enlightenment—it requires incarnation.

That is why this book insists on Jesus alone. Not because Christians are better or other faiths worthless, but because reality itself demands it. Sin is infinite offense against an infinite God. No finite creature can repair it. Only God could pay; only man should pay. In Jesus Christ, both meet—the debt is met, and death itself undone.

In the chapters ahead, we will move from the human predicament to the divine solution. We will see why no philosophy can substitute for revelation, why no moral effort can substitute for grace, and why the Cross, far from being an archaic symbol of cruelty, is the most rational and loving act imaginable. We will explore how the Incarnation reveals

INTRODUCTION

God's humility, how the Resurrection vindicates His truth, and how every competing claim of salvation falters before the empty tomb.

My aim is not to win arguments but to unveil reality. Christianity is not one religion among others; it is the story of God entering His own creation to redeem it. It does not compete with philosophies—it fulfills the longing behind them. If that claim sounds narrow, it is because truth is always narrow. Two plus two equals four, not anything we please. Love is exclusive by nature; a heart that loves all equally loves no one deeply.

This book was born out of conversations with friends, students, and skeptics who asked the same question in different ways: *Why Jesus?* I have seen sincere people chase meaning through crystals, therapy, self-help, and mysticism. I have seen Christians drift into a vague spirituality that worships feeling more than God. Beneath every attempt lies the same hunger: to be known, forgiven, and made whole. My prayer is that these pages will not merely defend doctrine but awaken wonder—that readers will see the logic and the love of a God who did not wait for us to reach Him but stepped into our darkness to lead us home.

There is still only one bridge across the abyss. It is made of wood and soaked in blood. Yet across it shines a light no darkness can overcome.

That light is Christ.

He is the Way.

1

The Human Condition: Why We Need Saving

Every serious question about God begins with a serious question about ourselves. Before we can ask *why Jesus*, we have to ask *why anyone needs saving at all.*

Our culture doesn't like that word — *saving*. It sounds dramatic, maybe even condescending. People today prefer to say they're "working on themselves," or "trying to be better," or "healing." But those phrases assume the problem is small enough to fix from within. They assume that if we could only think clearer, love harder, or behave better, the world would right itself.

And yet, it doesn't. No matter how much progress we make, evil outpaces us. Every century believes it has solved the last one's problems, and every new century proves it hasn't. We abolish slavery and invent exploitation. We create medicine and build bombs. We become more tolerant, and somehow more divided. The same sickness keeps returning under new names.

Something is wrong with the human condition that technology, philosophy, and politics cannot cure. The Bible calls that sickness *sin*, but sin doesn't just mean breaking rules. It means breaking communion. It means something has ruptured in the relationship between creation and its Creator — between life and the Source of life.

The story of Adam and Eve, whether one reads it as literal or symbolic, tells this truth with frightening clarity. God makes a world radiant with order and joy, places humanity in the center of it, and gives a single command not as a test of obedience but as a sign of relationship. "You may freely eat of every tree of the garden," He says, "but of the tree of the knowledge of good and evil you shall not eat." In other words: trust Me. Let Me be God, and you will flourish.

The serpent whispers the oldest lie in the universe: *You will not die.* Disobeying God, he suggests, is not rebellion but freedom. You can be your own source of truth, your own measure of good and evil. Humanity takes the bait — and for the first time, the world tastes death.

What really happens in that moment is not the breaking of a rule but the breaking of a bond. The connection between the creature and the Creator, between breath and its Giver, is severed. Imagine unplugging a lamp. The bulb still exists; the shape remains. But the light is gone. That is the human soul without God — intact but dark.

The problem isn't that humanity became *immoral*; it's that humanity became *mortal*. The fall from grace isn't merely a fall from innocence; it's a fall from life itself. Separation from the Source of Life is death, whether the heart stops beating or not.

This is why the story of Genesis rings true even in a scientific age. You don't need to believe in a literal garden to know that something in us has gone astray. We see it in every headline, every hospital ward, every human heart. We were made for love, yet we wound the people we love most. We long for peace, yet we start wars. We seek meaning, yet we fill our lives with noise. We know the good, yet we fail to do it.

No philosopher or scientist can deny this tension. Blaise Pascal called it the "greatness and wretchedness of man." We are noble enough to know we've fallen and broken enough not to stand up again. The world's moral teachers keep telling us to be good, but no one can explain why we aren't.

The atheist says it's ignorance; education will fix it. The sociologist says it's environment; reform will fix it. The therapist says it's trauma; healing will fix it. Each offers insight, and each falls short. We know more than any generation before us, and yet the heart of man remains the same.

That is because the problem isn't on the surface; it's in the roots. Sin is not simply an error in judgment; it's a wound in the soul. The tree still stands, but the roots have rotted. You can polish the leaves all you like — morality, culture, politics — but the decay keeps spreading because life no longer flows from the Source.

This is why the Christian faith insists on the need for salvation. It's not pessimism; it's realism. If the disease were ignorance, we'd need a teacher. If it were poverty, we'd need an economist. If it were loneliness, we'd need a friend. But if the disease is death, we need resurrection. Humanity isn't bad needing advice; it's dead needing life.

That truth, though hard, is liberating. It means we can stop pretending self-improvement will save us. It means our problem is not that we haven't tried hard enough but that we're trying to do the impossible — to live without the life of God. Every attempt at self-salvation ends in exhaustion, because it's the equivalent of a corpse trying to do push-ups.

The Bible describes this state with painful honesty: "You were dead in your trespasses and sins." Notice it doesn't say "wounded" or "struggling." It says *dead*. A dead body cannot revive itself; it can only receive life from outside. That's what grace is — life from outside.

Grace is God's own vitality, His presence, flowing back into a world that cut itself off. It's not just forgiveness for bad behaviour; it's resurrection for a dead soul. Grace doesn't excuse sin; it heals it. It doesn't overlook our failures; it transforms them.

That's why every other religion or philosophy, for all its wisdom, ultimately falls short. They can advise the sinner, but they cannot raise the dead. They can teach virtue, but they cannot restore communion. They can reform behaviour, but they cannot remake the heart.

To say this isn't arrogance — it's diagnosis. Humanity's sickness requires a supernatural cure, because the wound is supernatural in depth. If sin is separation from God, then salvation must be reunion with God. No amount of moral effort can substitute for divine intervention.

That's where Christianity begins — not with commandments but with a call: *"Come forth."* God's plan for the world is not moral reform but resurrection. But before we can understand how He accomplished it, we must understand what He was dealing with — a race that had lost its pulse and didn't know it.

We call that race *us*.

To understand the depth of what went wrong, we have to begin where most modern accounts stop: not with behaviour, but with being.

Sin is not first an act; it's a condition. It is what happens when the creature tries to live as though it were its own creator.

Every human life begins dependent — we need parents to conceive us, air to breathe, light to see. Yet, somehow, the adult heart rebels against this truth at its core. We want autonomy, the power to say, *I am my own source.* But there can be no self-sufficient creature; that is a contradiction in terms. To exist at all is to depend on something beyond ourselves.

That's why the original rebellion wasn't about fruit or forbidden knowledge. It was about independence. The human heart said, "I will define good and evil for myself." The result wasn't freedom; it was fragmentation. Relationship with God fractured, and everything else followed — man against woman, brother against brother, nation against nation, even man against the earth itself.

The ground, once meant to yield fruit effortlessly, now resists. Work becomes toil. Love becomes struggle. The world itself becomes a theatre of loss. Every grave, every war, every betrayal is an aftershock of that first quake. We feel it still, not as myth but as memory written in our nature.

People sometimes ask, "If God is good, why is there so much suffering?" The Christian answer is painful but honest: because creation has turned against its Creator. Evil isn't an equal power battling God; it's the absence of good, the rebellion of the finite against its own purpose. When we cut ourselves off from the Source of life, suffering is the shadow that follows.

That's why, even when we chase happiness, we end up restless. Augustine put it in one sentence that has never been improved: "Our hearts are restless until they rest in You." The ache of modern man — the anxiety that hums beneath our distractions — is that restlessness. We were built for the infinite and keep trying to fill the void with the finite.

That void explains why our brightest moments fade so fast. We invent wonders, yet we're bored. We achieve success, yet feel hollow. We fall in love, and still feel alone. Even our virtues betray us — the philanthropist grows proud, the reformer becomes cruel, the wise man turns cynical. No one escapes the fracture. The problem isn't that we do wrong things; it's that our nature itself is disordered.

The Bible calls this *original sin*, but the phrase can mislead. It doesn't mean we inherit guilt like a genetic defect. It means we're born into a broken relationship — a world already cut off from grace. Like children born in exile, we inherit the distance, not the blame. That's why sin is universal. We are all born into the same story — one that begins with alienation and ends, without intervention, in death.

But the Christian view of sin is not despairing. It is diagnostic. It names the wound so it can be healed. Only when we admit the disease can we seek the cure. And the first sign of recovery is humility — the recognition that we cannot save ourselves.

Modern culture finds that idea intolerable. We are trained from childhood to believe that everything depends on us: our happiness, our meaning, our salvation. But the Gospel begins where self-help ends. It says: stop trying to fix what only God can raise.

This is why moralism — the belief that being good is enough — fails. It confuses the symptom with the cause. It's like giving vitamins to a corpse. The corpse may look more dignified, but it remains dead. Ethics can make us respectable; only grace can make us alive.

That's what Scripture means when it contrasts *flesh* and *spirit*. "Flesh" doesn't mean the body; it means life lived apart from God, life curved in on itself. It is self-reliance dressed as virtue. The modern world celebrates the flesh — autonomy, self-expression, self-creation — but these are only the old rebellion with a marketing team. We tell ourselves we are free, yet we are addicted, anxious, and lonely. The soul cannot feed on itself.

Even religion can become fleshly when it turns into performance — doing good deeds to earn divine approval rather than to receive divine life. The Pharisees in the Gospels were not wicked men; they were moral perfectionists. But morality without grace produces pride, not holiness. The human race has tried both rebellion and religion, and neither has worked. Both start from man's side of the chasm. What's needed must come from the other side.

This is where the concept of *grace* enters — perhaps the most misunderstood word in the Christian vocabulary. Grace is not permission to sin, nor a sentimental feeling of being accepted. Grace is the power of divine life entering human weakness. It's not God saying, "I forgive you; carry on." It's God saying, "I forgive you; rise."

To grasp grace, picture a lifeless heart restarting under defibrillation. That jolt is not earned; it's given. The patient doesn't contribute; he receives. That's what grace does to the human soul. It brings it back to life. "While we were yet sinners," Paul writes, "Christ died for us." The initiative is always divine.

Grace doesn't compete with effort; it precedes it. Once revived, the patient can breathe and move again. That's why Christian holiness is not effort trying to achieve life but life expressing itself through effort. Good works don't create grace; they reveal it.

This is what separates Christianity from every other moral or religious system. All others tell man what he must do to reach God. Christianity tells what God has done to reach man. The Law points upward; the Cross reaches downward. The ladder is broken; so Heaven descends.

Before we move to that descent, we must linger a little longer on the truth it responds to: humanity apart from God is not ill, but dead. And only the Author of Life can write resurrection into our story.

The first step toward healing is honesty. Until we see the human condition clearly, the Gospel will sound like exaggeration. Only the sick understand medicine; only the drowning understand rescue.

We have learned to rename sin until it feels manageable. Pride becomes self-confidence. Greed becomes ambition. Lust becomes self-expression. Envy becomes drive. Sloth becomes rest. Anger becomes passion. The words change; the wound remains.

But deep down, we know something is wrong. The evidence is everywhere — in the world and in us. We see war and corruption on the news, yet the same war rages in our own hearts. We want good but end up serving evil. We condemn lies and then tell them. We decry greed and then feed it. We want peace but cannot stop fighting, even with ourselves.

This is what Paul meant when he wrote: "I do not do the good I want, but the evil I do not want is what I keep on doing." That confession has never been outdated. It describes the human heart precisely. Something has snapped between knowing the good and doing it. We possess reason, will, and conscience, but they no longer align. The mind knows, the heart wants, and the will falters.

The ancient philosophers saw this too. Socrates said that no one knowingly does evil — that if people understood the good, they would always choose it. But history disproves him. Knowledge alone doesn't save. We know what is right and still resist it. The failure runs deeper than ignorance. It's bondage.

The human will is not neutral, balancing good and evil on equal scales. It is tilted inward. We are born self-absorbed — not necessarily malicious, but curved toward ourselves. That is the essence of sin: not merely doing bad things but *being centered on me*. Even when we act generously, we often do it for pride, comfort, or reputation. We are addicted to the self.

This addiction is invisible because it's universal. Like air, it surrounds us so completely we no longer notice it. Modern culture even celebrates it as virtue. "Follow your heart." "Be true to yourself." "You do you." Yet Scripture warns, "The heart is deceitful above all things." The self we are told to trust is the very thing that keeps us enslaved.

And so, despite all our sophistication, the world still looks strangely like Genesis 3. We invent tools and call them progress, but the same desires drive them — control, autonomy, mastery. We build towers of technology and ideology, promising unity, and end up scattering again. We are the same builders of Babel with better materials.

But the Bible does not speak of this condition to humiliate us. It names the disease so we can seek the cure. Grace begins with truth. The more we understand our helplessness, the more we become capable of receiving help. Pride is the only obstacle to salvation, because pride insists, "I can fix this myself."

When Scripture says, "All have sinned and fall short of the glory of God," it's not condemning humanity; it's diagnosing reality. Falling short doesn't just mean missing the target of moral perfection. It means missing the purpose for which we were made: to share God's glory, to reflect His love, to live in His life. A mirror that refuses the light no longer fulfills its nature.

That's why sin is both tragedy and treason. Tragedy, because it destroys what is most beautiful in us. Treason, because it turns our freedom against its Giver. Every lie, every lust, every act of cruelty is a rebellion against love itself. And because love is what holds the universe together, rebellion against love is rebellion against life.

It's important to grasp this before talking about salvation. Salvation doesn't mean God deciding to be lenient. It means God deciding to recreate. The Cross isn't divine paperwork clearing our record; it's divine surgery restoring our nature. The wound was mortal; the cure must be miraculous.

This is what makes Christianity both humbling and hopeful. It humbles us by showing we cannot save ourselves, and it fills us with hope because Someone can. Grace doesn't flatter the ego; it replaces it with gratitude.

Think of the difference between *good advice* and *good news*. Every religion and philosophy gives advice — how to live, how to pray, how to think. Advice assumes we can act on it. News tells what has already been done. The Gospel is not advice. It's news. "For while we were helpless, at the right time Christ died for the ungodly."

Before the news makes sense, we must admit the helplessness. A man who believes he is swimming will never reach for the lifeguard. The modern world keeps pretending to swim — through science, through politics, through therapy. All these can improve conditions in the water, but none can change the fact that we're sinking. The soul cannot tread water forever.

Christianity dares to look reality in the face. It says: Yes, the world is beautiful, but it's broken. Yes, humanity is noble, but it's fallen. Yes, love exists, but it dies. The solution must address that paradox. A perfect lawgiver can't fix it. A prophet can't fix it. A new philosophy can't fix it. Only resurrection can.

And resurrection requires death first — death to pride, to illusion, to the fantasy of self-sufficiency. Only when the old self dies can grace raise something new. The Gospel is not about self-improvement but self-replacement: "It is no longer I who live, but Christ who lives in me."

If we can see this, we're ready to understand everything that follows. The Old Testament's strange rituals, the sacrifices, the commandments — all were early treatments, partial measures pointing toward the final cure. Humanity's story is the story of a patient in intensive care being kept alive until the surgeon arrives.

And He has arrived. But before we meet Him, we must understand what He came to heal: not simply guilt, but death itself.

Death, in the biblical sense, is not merely the moment the heart stops beating. It is separation — the soul cut off from the Source of life. That is what happened in Eden, and it is what happens in every age when humanity insists on self-sufficiency. We exist, but we no longer live. We move, think, build, and create, yet all under the shadow of mortality. Our greatest triumphs still end in funerals.

That is why the Bible speaks of two kinds of death — physical and spiritual. Physical death is inevitable; spiritual death is optional. The first ends life in the body, the second ends life in the soul. And the latter is the deeper tragedy, because it can happen long before the grave. You can be breathing and still be dead inside.

We sense this instinctively. We try to fill the void with substitutes: romance, success, wealth, recognition. But the more we feed the hunger, the stronger it grows. What we crave isn't pleasure but permanence. We want something that doesn't fade when the lights go out. Every act of idolatry — whether it's worshiping power, beauty, or self — is an attempt to satisfy that eternal longing with something temporary.

Saint Augustine understood this better than most. In his *Confessions*, he writes about chasing satisfaction through ambition, sensuality, and philosophy, only to find emptiness at the end of every road. His turning point came when he realised that nothing created could satisfy a heart made for the Creator. "You have made us for Yourself," he prayed, "and our hearts are restless until they rest in You."

Restlessness is the key word. It's not a mood but a symptom — the symptom of a soul dislocated from its home. Just as pain warns of injury, spiritual restlessness warns of separation from God. The ache of the human heart is proof that we were made for more than this world can give.

Even our conscience points to this. Every culture, from the dawn of civilisation, recognises moral law — honour your parents, do not steal, do not murder, keep your word. These universal instincts are not inventions of religion; they are traces of the divine image still glowing in fallen humanity. But conscience, though real, is powerless to save. It can accuse or excuse, but it cannot absolve. It can tell us that we're sick, but it cannot make us well.

That's why guilt — though uncomfortable — is actually a grace. It's the soul's pain receptors. A person without guilt is like a body without nerves: unable to feel, and therefore unable to heal. The tragedy of our time is not that people feel guilty, but that they no longer know why. We have guilt without God, shame without forgiveness. We sense that something's wrong, but we no longer know where to bring it.

Every failed attempt at redemption — every ideology, therapy, or revolution that promises utopia — is an attempt to deal with guilt without grace. But it cannot be done. When a society denies sin, it does not remove guilt; it multiplies it. We see this today in our obsession with virtue signalling, cancel culture, and moral outrage. We have replaced confession with accusation. The hunger for righteousness remains, but we no longer have an altar.

The story of human history could be summarised in one phrase: *the search for a lost altar.* We were created to worship, and when we forget God, we don't stop worshipping — we just change the object. We turn our hearts toward idols of our own making: money, sex, politics, power. The human heart is an altar that will burn for something. The only question is whether what it burns for will give life or consume it.

That's why idolatry, in Scripture, is not just a primitive superstition but a psychological truth. To love anything more than God is to give it power to destroy you. When we make success our god, failure becomes our hell. When we make pleasure our god, pain becomes our hell. When we make self our god, every limit becomes unbearable. The heart that worships the wrong thing eventually breaks under the weight of its own devotion.

This explains why even good things, without God, eventually enslave us. Family, work, country, even love — all are good in themselves, but when treated as ultimate, they crush us. No finite thing can carry the infinite weight of meaning. Only God can.

At its core, then, sin is disordered love. We do not stop loving when we fall — we simply love in the wrong order. We love creation above the Creator, gifts above Giver, self above truth. Grace does not erase love; it restores its order. It teaches us to love God first so that everything else can be loved rightly.

This is why Jesus later called the greatest commandment not "obey perfectly" but "love the Lord your God with all your heart, soul, mind, and strength." The problem with humanity is not too much love, but too little of the right kind. And since our hearts have lost their compass, no moral reform can fix the direction. We need something stronger than willpower — we need new hearts.

That is precisely what God promised through the prophet Ezekiel:

"I will remove from you your heart of stone and give you a heart of flesh. I will put my Spirit within you and cause you to walk in my ways." This is not poetry; it's prophecy. It names what only grace can do — change us from the inside out.

But before the Spirit could dwell in man, sin had to be dealt with. The barrier had to be broken, the debt paid, the wound healed. That is why all the history of Israel — the sacrifices, the temple, the prophets — existed: to prepare the world for the cure.

The Law was never meant to save; it was meant to reveal the need for saving. Like an X-ray, it exposes what lies beneath the surface. "Through the law comes knowledge of sin," Paul writes. Israel's story is our story — humanity discovering that no amount of external effort can make a heart clean. The Law could restrain evil but not erase it. It could prescribe sacrifice but not provide the final one.

The old covenant was God's way of teaching us our dependency. The sacrifices cried out: "We need atonement." The prophets cried out: "We need renewal." Every altar pointed forward to one final act where God Himself would provide the Lamb.

But that comes later in the story. For now, we stand where Israel once stood — aware of our slavery, longing for freedom, yet powerless to achieve it. We have learned that sin is more than bad choices; it's a broken nature. And a broken nature cannot repair itself.

Only the Maker can restore what He made.

Every human heart knows what it means to long for freedom and yet find the same chains waiting every morning. The ancient Israelites learned that in Egypt. We learn it in our own hearts. The Pharaoh that enslaves us is not a tyrant outside but a power within — sin's rule, subtle but total. We know we're enslaved when even our best intentions betray us.

This is why the story of Exodus mirrors the story of every soul. Egypt represents bondage, the wilderness represents struggle, and the

Promised Land represents communion — life with God. But no one crosses that desert by willpower. It takes deliverance, not discipline. The Hebrews could not free themselves from Pharaoh; God had to send a deliverer. And the same pattern repeats in salvation history: humanity cries, God descends, grace acts.

The mistake of every age is to believe that we can free ourselves by new commandments. We pass laws, invent philosophies, create ideologies — and yet the chains remain. The oppressor just changes shape. The external Egypts of the past have become internal now: addiction, anxiety, the tyranny of self-image, the endless hunger for approval. Sin is slavery dressed in the clothes of freedom.

The irony of sin is that it always promises autonomy and always delivers bondage. We chase pleasure to feel alive and end up numb. We grasp control to feel safe and end up fearful. We pursue self-expression and end up isolated. Every sin is a deal with the serpent: "You shall be as gods," he says, but the small print reads, "and you shall die like men."

It is hard to admit this because it strikes at our pride. We prefer to think of sin as something external — the violence, corruption, and cruelty of others. But Scripture points the finger inward: "All have sinned." The line between good and evil does not run between nations or classes; it runs down the center of every human heart.

Even our goodness is compromised. That's what Augustine meant when he said the virtues of pagans, however noble, were still "splendid vices." They glimmered with moral beauty but were rooted in self-love rather than divine love. A man may give to charity for recognition, speak truth for pride, die for honour. Virtue without grace remains self-serving — a polished idol of the self.

That doesn't mean there's no goodness outside faith. It means even our goodness needs redemption. We are not neutral beings who occasionally sin; we are wounded beings whose every act bears the mark of that wound. The image of God in us is not destroyed, but it's distorted — like a masterpiece slashed by a vandal. The painting is still beautiful, but the scars are unmistakable.

This explains why every attempt to build a perfect society ends in disappointment. We imagine that if only systems were fairer, education broader, and resources shared, evil would vanish. But evil keeps reinventing itself because it lives inside the human heart. As long as hearts remain unhealed, even the best systems will corrode. That is why the Gospel does not start with politics or psychology but with the person. Salvation is not social engineering; it's heart surgery.

The prophets saw this clearly. Jeremiah wrote, "Can the Ethiopian change his skin or the leopard its spots? Then also you can do good who are accustomed to do evil." The point was not racial or moral despair — it was metaphysical realism. A nature cannot transform itself; it must be transformed. The leopard needs a new nature; the sinner needs a new heart.

That new heart is the promise of grace, but before we reach grace, we must face the consequence of its absence: death. "The wages of sin is death," Paul says. That isn't divine revenge; it's cause and effect. To cut yourself off from the Source of life is to die, just as a flower cut from the root withers even in sunlight.

This death, spiritual and physical, is the universal inheritance of Adam. It's what theologians call *original sin*, but we can think of it as the world's spiritual DNA — a mutation passed from generation to generation. The evidence is undeniable: no one needs to be taught selfishness. Children hoard toys before they can speak. Civilizations collapse into cruelty as soon as they gain power. We repeat the same cycle as though it were genetic memory. It is.

Original sin doesn't mean we are born evil; it means we are born disconnected. Humanity is like a tree with cut roots — still green for a time, still capable of producing leaves, but destined for decay unless grafted back into life. That grafting is grace, and the root we must be joined to is Christ. But before the graft can happen, the wound must be cleaned — sin exposed, pride cut away, humility learned.

It's tempting to soften this truth. Many modern thinkers try to reinterpret the Fall as mere myth, a metaphor for human maturity or evolution. But the persistence of evil proves otherwise. There is nothing metaphorical about Auschwitz, about abuse, about betrayal. Evil is not simply ignorance; it is rebellion — the misuse of freedom against its Maker. Only a real fall can explain the depth of the world's ruin.

And if the Fall is real, then redemption must be real too — not an idea, but an event. Christianity insists on both: a real wound, a real cure. If sin were just ignorance, we would need enlightenment. If it were merely weakness, we would need therapy. But because it is death, we need resurrection. The cure must match the disease.

That's what sets Christianity apart. The Gospel doesn't offer a philosophy of life; it offers the invasion of Life itself. It doesn't tell us to improve our condition; it tells us our condition is terminal and that the Physician has entered the room. Grace doesn't polish; it resurrects.

To understand salvation, then, we must see the world as Scripture sees it — not as a hospital for the sick improving day by day, but as a morgue where the dead are waiting for a voice to call them forth. And that voice must be divine.

The same Word that said "Let there be light" in creation must one day say "Let there be life" in redemption. That moment — when the Word Himself enters the world He made — is the hinge of all history. It's the answer to every myth, every philosophy, every longing.

But we are not there yet. For now, the diagnosis stands: humanity, separated from God, is not just limping; it's lifeless. The next chapter will show what happens when the Author of life writes Himself into the story.

The story of the Fall is not a tale of primitive superstition; it is the most profound psychological and spiritual diagnosis ever written. It tells us that the human problem is not external but internal, not circumstantial but essential. We are not simply creatures who *make* mistakes; we are creatures who *are* mistaken — misaligned from the purpose for which we were created.

When Scripture says we were made "in the image and likeness of God," it means something extraordinary: that human beings were designed to reflect God's own life into creation. We were meant to be living mirrors of divine love, icons of the infinite. Sin shattered that mirror. The fragments remain — each capable of reflecting a sliver of beauty — but none alone shows the whole face. The world's religions and philosophies are, in a sense, those scattered fragments trying to reconstruct the image.

This is why, even in its brokenness, humanity cannot forget God. We may deny Him, debate Him, or replace Him, but we cannot erase Him. The memory of Eden is buried too deep. The longing for transcendence, the instinct for morality, the craving for eternal meaning — all these are echoes of a design we can neither fully recall nor fully destroy. As Ecclesiastes says, "God has set eternity in the human heart."

But eternity cannot be contained by a finite heart. That's the source of both our greatness and our misery. Every human achievement, from philosophy to art to science, bears witness to that restless desire to touch something beyond ourselves. Yet the very desire proves our dependence. The fact that we yearn for the infinite is evidence that we are not it.

The tragedy is that, left on our own, that yearning turns inward. We build idols out of the very gifts meant to lead us back to God. Knowledge, beauty, power — all become substitutes for the One they were meant to reveal. The devil's subtlest lie is not "there is no God," but "you can be like God." Not in holiness, but in autonomy. Not as child to Father, but as rival to rival.

This rebellion is what Christian theology calls *pride*, and pride is not merely vanity — it's the root of every sin. It's the declaration of independence from the Source of being. Pride says, "I owe nothing, I need nothing, I define everything." It's the voice that echoes still in every human age, even in our virtues. We serve others to feel righteous, seek justice to feel superior, love to be loved. Even our goodness is infected with self.

And so the question must be asked: can a race this curved inward ever straighten itself? Can the mirror repair its own fracture?

Every attempt at self-redemption says yes. The modern world is full of these attempts. We see it in the cult of progress — the belief that time itself will heal us. But time heals nothing; it only hides wounds under new names. We see it in the cult of psychology — the belief that by understanding ourselves we can save ourselves. But introspection without grace is a hall of mirrors: you see endlessly, but you never escape. We see it in the cult of activism — the belief that if we fix society, the soul will follow. But no social reform can cure original sin. You can build a perfect system, and still find corruption inside the human heart that runs it.

The most dangerous illusion of all is the religious one: that we can climb to God by moral effort. This was the temptation of the Pharisees, and it remains ours. We think we can barter with God through good works, as though heaven were a wage to be earned. But love cannot be bought; it can only be received.

This is why, from Genesis onward, God's relationship with humanity is described not as a contract but as a *covenant.* A contract exchanges goods; a covenant exchanges selves. The purpose of religion was never to build a ladder to heaven but to restore communion — to bind God and man again in love. Yet even that covenant, written on tablets of stone, could not change the heart of stone. Something more intimate, more radical, was required.

Through prophets like Jeremiah and Ezekiel, God promised exactly that: a new covenant, written not on stone but on the heart; not law imposed from outside but life infused from within. "I will put my law within them, and I will write it upon their hearts," God said. That is the prophecy of grace.

But before grace could enter, justice had to be satisfied. The fracture could not simply be ignored. For love to be truly just, it must take sin seriously. This is why the Old Testament sacrifices existed — not to appease a capricious deity, but to dramatize the cost of reconciliation. Every drop of blood on those ancient altars was a foreshadowing of what sin costs and what grace would one day pay.

We often imagine that God's justice and mercy are opposites, but they are not. They are two sides of the same coin: God's unwavering love for what is good. Mercy is justice bending down to lift us up, and justice is mercy refusing to pretend evil doesn't matter. Both require the same thing — the restoration of the broken relationship between holiness and humanity.

This is the heart of why self-help fails. It assumes that the problem is behavioural and that forgiveness is enough. But forgiveness without transformation is not salvation; it's sentimentality. If a murderer is merely pardoned but not changed, justice is not done and love is not restored. The human soul needs more than acquittal — it needs resurrection.

The first part of God's plan, therefore, was to teach humanity what sin really is: not merely offence against law but rupture in life. Every commandment, every prophet, every exile and return was a rehearsal for the final act — the descent of grace into flesh.

Before that moment, the human race stood like Israel in exile: aware of its slavery, aware of its need, but powerless to escape. The prophets had promised deliverance; philosophers had guessed at a higher truth;

myth had dreamed of dying gods and rising life. All of them were shadows waiting for substance.

And then, at the turning point of time, the Author entered His own story.

When God entered His creation, He didn't come as a storm, or as an idea, or as a new law. He came as a child.

The simplicity of that moment hides the depth of its meaning. The Creator took on the nature of the creature who had rebelled against Him. The divine Word through whom the galaxies were made chose to learn how to speak, to eat, to suffer, to die. Why? Because the problem He came to heal wasn't ignorance, but estrangement.

The Incarnation is not a strange appendix to human history; it is its hinge. Everything before it points toward it, and everything after it flows from it. If the human story is a long exile, the Incarnation is the moment the King steps into the wilderness to lead His people home.

But to understand why such a drastic act was needed, we must remember how deep the wound runs. Sin didn't merely offend God's honour — it distorted the whole fabric of reality. When humanity turned away from the Giver of life, death entered everything: not just human souls, but creation itself. The thorns that choke the ground, the entropy that pulls all things toward decay — these are not punishments arbitrarily imposed; they are the echo of disconnection.

That is why Scripture says "the whole creation groans." The universe itself is waiting for reconciliation. The Incarnation, then, isn't only about rescuing individual souls; it's about healing the cosmos from the inside out.

Still, before the world could be restored, humanity had to be reconciled with its Maker. But who could bridge that gap?

Man owed the debt; only man could repay it. Yet the debt was infinite, because it was owed to an infinite God. No finite creature could balance the scales. The only solution was for God Himself to enter humanity — to pay the debt from our side, in our nature, by His own divine life.

This is why no prophet, no sage, no philosopher could suffice. Their words might inspire, but they could not transform. Only the union of divine and human in one Person could heal what had been torn apart. The Incarnation is not one religious myth among many; it is metaphysical necessity. It is the only possible meeting point between infinite holiness and finite sinfulness.

Think of humanity as a broken instrument. Every other religion tries to retune the strings. Christianity says the Musician Himself picked up the instrument and played His song through it again. The melody restored the harmony.

But for that music to sound, the strings had to be stretched, and the wood had to be broken. That breaking happened on the Cross. There, the consequences of sin — separation, suffering, death — were absorbed by the very One who alone was innocent. The punishment was not imposed from outside; it was embraced from within. Love took responsibility for what justice required.

That's why the Cross is not a symbol of cruelty but of realism. It shows that love is not sentiment but sacrifice. It shows that God takes evil seriously enough to destroy it, not by violence but by mercy. Only divine love could go that far — to take the place of the guilty, to enter the very depths of human despair and fill it with His presence.

Every other system says, "Here is what you must do to reach God."

The Gospel says, "Here is what God has done to reach you."

And this is the final proof that humanity cannot save itself: even when God stood among us, healing the sick and raising the dead, we nailed Him to a tree. That is the measure of our blindness — and the measure of His love. The very rejection became redemption. The hammer that drove the nails built the bridge.

The Incarnation is the answer to the human condition because it takes the human condition into God. The Creator doesn't just fix His creation from a distance; He joins it, bears it, transforms it. "The Word became flesh," John writes, "and dwelt among us." The Greek literally says, *He pitched His tent among us.* The God who once dwelled in the tabernacle of Israel now tabernacles in human flesh. The presence once confined to a temple now walks the dusty roads of Galilee.

This is why Christianity cannot be reduced to ethics or inspiration. It is ontological — a change in being. The gulf between God and man no longer defines reality; the union of God and man does. What was impossible by nature becomes possible by grace.

Grace, then, is not a thing God gives; it is God giving Himself. It's not a divine favour sprinkled over good people; it's the divine life poured into dead people. The Cross and Resurrection are the means by which that life is made available to us.

Without the Incarnation, religion remains man's search for God. With it, salvation becomes God's search for man. That is the crucial reversal. The lost sheep cannot find the shepherd; the shepherd must come looking.

But if that's true, then the first step of faith is not achievement but surrender. Christianity begins not with "I will," but with "Help me." It's the recognition that our efforts to fix the human condition have failed, and that grace alone can lift us.

That is what baptism later signifies — death to the old life and rebirth into the new. The same pattern that defines Christ's story — death and resurrection — becomes the pattern of every believer's story. Salvation is not escape from the human condition; it's the transfiguration of it. The same flesh that sinned is now indwelt by Spirit; the same body that dies will one day rise.

This is the astonishing logic of the Gospel: God does not destroy what is broken; He heals it from the inside. The divine doesn't replace the human; it redeems it. The Incarnation is not God's rejection of creation but His endorsement of it — proof that what He made is still worth saving.

The entire Christian faith, then, rests on this claim: that the God who is life entered death so that death might collapse from within. That's not poetry; it's the mechanics of redemption. Only infinite life can absorb infinite loss.

And so, the story that began in a garden ends on a hill — and begins again in an empty tomb. The human condition meets its cure not in philosophy, not in morality, but in a Person. The same Word who said, "Let there be light" now says, "Come forth."

To grasp how complete this healing is, we must see that Jesus didn't come merely to reverse Adam's failure but to fulfill humanity's purpose. He didn't just repair what was lost; He raised it to a higher level than before. The Son of God became the Son of Man so that the sons of men could become sons of God.

That is the end of the story that began in Eden — not simply restoration, but glorification. Humanity was made for communion, not competition, with the divine. Our destiny was never to be independent creatures managing our own morality, but children sharing in the Father's life. The Incarnation isn't a detour in history; it is the revelation of what creation was always meant to become.

The first Adam tried to seize divinity and fell; the second Adam, Christ, received humanity and lifted it back to God. What was once a chasm is now a bridge. Grace doesn't erase nature; it perfects it. That's why every act of authentic Christianity begins with receiving before doing — because the Gospel is not about self-improvement, it's about self-participation in divine life.

When Scripture calls Jesus "the new Adam," it means that in Him, the human story restarts. Where the first Adam grasped, the second obeyed. Where the first hid in shame, the second stretched out His arms in surrender. The old humanity, turned inward on itself, died with Him; the new humanity, turned outward toward the Father, rose with Him.

That is the key to understanding why Christianity insists there is only one way to God — not because God is narrow, but because reality itself has only one centre. The human problem is not lack of knowledge or morality; it's disconnection from life itself. And life has one source. You cannot plug into an alternate sun or breathe an alternative oxygen. "In Him we live and move and have our being."

Every moral system, every religion, every act of kindness still draws its goodness from that single light. But unless that light enters the heart — unless grace reconnects the soul to the Source — the current does not flow. Christianity is not exclusionary; it is explanatory. It names the truth already written into creation: only union with the Giver of Life can restore life.

This is why, even for those who do not yet know Christ, their every movement toward truth and love is already a movement toward Him. He is the gravitational centre of goodness itself. When a scientist pursues truth, a mother sacrifices for her child, or a pagan prays to the unknown God, they are all, in some hidden way, responding to the pull of the same grace. The difference is that in Jesus, the grace becomes visible and personal. The longing of the ages acquires a name and a face.

And yet, this revelation confronts each of us with a choice. If the diagnosis is true — if sin is death — then no neutral ground remains. We either receive life or reject it. The Cross divides history because it reveals that God's mercy is total, but not automatic. He will not force us to live.

The tragedy of sin is not that God refuses to forgive; it's that man refuses to be healed. Like Adam hiding in the garden, we still run from the very Presence that could restore us. Pride whispers that we're fine as we are, that we can fix ourselves, that we don't need grace. But pride is simply death wearing perfume. It smells pleasant for a while, and then the rot sets in.

That is why the first act of faith is humility — not grovelling, but honesty. To say, "I need saving" is not weakness; it's the beginning of wisdom. It's the moment the soul opens the window and light rushes in. Grace can only fill what empties itself.

The rest of the Christian story — the Cross, the Resurrection, the Church — flows from this recognition. Everything that follows in this book builds on this first truth: humanity without God is not limping but lifeless, and God, in Jesus Christ, has entered the grave to bring us back to life.

This is the ground zero of salvation. Until we see that, Christianity will seem unnecessary — just another moral option. But when we do see it, everything else falls into place. The Incarnation, the Crucifixion, the Resurrection — they're no longer strange doctrines but the only logical answers to the human condition.

If the human story is a fall from life, then salvation must be the return of life. If the wound is death, then the cure is resurrection. And if grace is life restored, then faith is simply the act of breathing again.

All that remains is to decide whether we will inhale.

2

The Old Covenant: How God Began to Reach Us

The story of salvation does not begin in Bethlehem. It begins in a desert, with an old man named Abram and a voice that called him out of nowhere. "Go from your country and your kindred and your father's house to the land that I will show you." Those words mark the first step in God's long rescue mission — His slow self-revelation to a world that had forgotten His face.

The human race had fallen, but God had not given up. The story of the Old Testament is not about a wrathful deity inventing rules; it's about a faithful God pursuing His runaway children. The covenant with Israel is the history of divine patience. Like a father stooping to speak the language of his child, God begins by meeting humanity where it is — tribal, fearful, surrounded by idols — and begins to teach them what He is really like.

At the dawn of Genesis, humanity knew of God but did not *know* Him. The fragments of memory from Eden lived on as myths scattered across the nations — stories of creation, flood, sacrifice, gods who die and rise. They were faint echoes of a truth the world had lost. The human imagination, cut off from revelation, turned those echoes into idols. The one Creator became a pantheon of powers. The divine image in man became blurred beyond recognition.

So God began to reintroduce Himself. He chose one man, not because Abram was special, but because love always begins personally. "I will make of you a great nation," God said, "and through you all families of the earth shall be blessed." From the start, the plan was universal. God was not creating a club; He was crafting a vessel — a people through whom His light could reach everyone.

Abraham's story is the beginning of faith because it begins with trust. He leaves his homeland with no map, no proof, only a promise. In him we see the first reversal of Adam's sin. Where Adam doubted God's goodness, Abraham believes it. Where Adam grasped, Abraham surrenders. That is why he is called "the father of faith."

The covenant God makes with him is not a contract but a relationship sealed in blood. God walks between the torn pieces of sacrifice Himself, saying, in essence, "If I am unfaithful to this promise, let what happened to these animals happen to Me." The Creator binds Himself to His creature. This is the shocking humility of divine love: the infinite pledging Himself to the finite, the faithful promising Himself to the faithless.

That is the pattern of the entire Old Testament. Each covenant — with Noah, Abraham, Moses, David — builds on the one before it, widening the circle of grace. Noah's covenant restores creation after the flood. Abraham's forms a people. Moses' forms a nation. David's forms a kingdom. Each reveals a little more of God's heart.

At Sinai, that heart speaks in thunder and fire, but beneath the terror is tenderness. The Ten Commandments are not arbitrary decrees; they are the charter of a people learning to live free. The Israelites had been slaves for four hundred years — they knew only the voice of Pharaoh. When God gives the Law, He is teaching them what it means to be human again. "I am the Lord your God who brought you out of the house of slavery." Before any commandment comes a declaration of relationship. The Law begins with grace.

To modern ears, commandments sound restrictive. But to a people fresh from bondage, they were liberation. Each "you shall not" was a reminder that their worth no longer depended on Pharaoh's whip. "You shall not kill" — because life is sacred, not property. "You shall not covet" — because you are no longer defined by what you lack. "Remember the Sabbath" — because you are not slaves; you can rest.

The Law was God's way of reordering human desire, of training the heart in trust. It wasn't meant to replace relationship but to protect it. Just as traffic rules don't imprison drivers but make travel possible, the commandments created a space where freedom could flourish. God was teaching Israel what Adam refused to learn — that true freedom is not independence from God but dependence on Him.

Still, the Law by itself could not heal the human heart. It could restrain sin but not remove it. It could reveal the shape of holiness but not supply the strength to achieve it. It was a mirror, not medicine. That's why, woven through the Law, God introduced sacrifice — the visible sign of invisible grace.

Sacrifice, in ancient religion, was everywhere. Pagans offered animals, crops, even humans to appease their gods. But in Israel, sacrifice was transformed. It was no longer a bribe to angry deities; it became a language of love and repentance. The blood of lambs and bulls was a reminder that sin costs life, that broken communion cannot be mended without gift. Each offering on the altar was a symbol of the truth that would one day take flesh — "without the shedding of blood, there is no forgiveness of sins."

But the prophets knew that these sacrifices were not the end. "I desire mercy, not sacrifice," God said through Hosea. The ritual was never meant to satisfy Him but to point beyond itself — to the day when He Himself would provide the lamb. Abraham had glimpsed it on Mount Moriah when God stayed his hand and supplied a ram. Every altar after that looked forward to another mountain, another Lamb.

Israel's story, then, is not about divine partiality but preparation. God was not playing favourites; He was building foundations. He revealed Himself to one nation so that, through them, the nations could be healed. Their history was a classroom for the world — their faith a rehearsal for the Gospel.

Through centuries of covenant, commandment, and prophecy, God was teaching humanity two truths: that sin separates, and that He will not rest until the separation ends. Each promise deepened the revelation. The one true God was not distant like the idols; He was personal, faithful, and passionately involved in history. He entered covenants not out of need but out of love — love that always takes initiative, always stoops, always calls.

By the time the prophets appeared, Israel had learned to name that love: *hesed* — steadfast mercy, covenantal faithfulness. It is the word that sums up the Old Testament's God — not an impersonal force, but a heart that refuses to give up. Even when His people betrayed Him, He chased them like a husband pursuing an unfaithful bride. "How can I give you up, O Ephraim?" He cries through Hosea. The God of Israel is not the God of the philosophers; He is a lover with wounds.

The world did not know it yet, but those wounds would one day be literal.

If Genesis tells the story of humanity's fall, Exodus begins the story of God's response. The descendants of Abraham had become slaves in Egypt—oppressed, voiceless, forgotten. Yet in the midst of their suffering, God remembered His promise. The cry of His people rose up, and the Lord revealed Himself anew: not as a distant deity, but as *I AM*—the living, personal God who hears, sees, and acts.

When God spoke to Moses from the burning bush, He gave a name that no pagan god had ever dared to claim. The gods of the nations were forces, concepts, projections of human fear and desire. But *I AM WHO I AM* was something else entirely—existence itself, Being made personal. This was the first unveiling of divine intimacy: not an idea about God, but God introducing Himself.

"I have seen the misery of My people... I have come down to deliver them." Those words set the tone for the rest of salvation history. Every act that follows—the plagues, the parting of the sea, the manna, the commandments—is an unfolding of that single promise: *I have come down.* Christianity begins there, not in human ascent but divine descent.

The Exodus is not just ancient history; it is the blueprint for salvation. Pharaoh's Egypt is the world of sin and slavery. Moses is the mediator pointing toward the true Deliverer. The Red Sea is baptism, the crossing from bondage to freedom. The desert is the testing of faith. The Promised Land is communion with God. In Israel's physical journey, God was sketching the spiritual journey of every soul.

When the Israelites reached Sinai, they were not just freed slaves—they were a nation being betrothed. The covenant at Sinai was a marriage ceremony. God spoke His vows: "I will be your God, and you will be My people." The thunder and lightning were not signs of wrath but of awe. The mountain trembled because heaven was touching earth.

Then came the Law, which Christians so often misunderstand. It was not given to crush Israel under impossible demands but to teach them what freedom means. They had left Pharaoh's chains, but Pharaoh still lived in their hearts. Freedom without formation always decays into chaos. The Law was God's way of shaping a people capable of love.

Every commandment begins from relationship. "You shall have no other gods before Me" is not jealousy—it's fidelity. "Do not steal," "Do not kill," "Do not commit adultery" are not arbitrary moral codes—they protect love. The Law is divine wisdom translated into human life.

But the Israelites, like the rest of us, struggled to live it. They believed obedience could be traded for blessing, as though holiness were a contract. When they obeyed, they prospered; when they disobeyed, they suffered. Yet the deeper truth—the one God kept teaching through their history—was that obedience was not a transaction but a participation in life itself. The Law was never meant to save; it was meant to point to the Saviour.

That is why God sent prophets. They were not fortune tellers but truth tellers, calling Israel back to the heart of the covenant. Again and again, the prophets reminded the people that God's desire was not ritual precision but transformed hearts. "This people honours Me with their lips," Isaiah thundered, "but their hearts are far from Me." Micah asked, "What does the Lord require of you but to do justice, love mercy, and walk humbly with your God?"

The prophets were like doctors diagnosing a patient who mistook symptoms for health. Israel thought religion was enough; the prophets said repentance was required. When they warned of exile, they weren't predicting punishment but describing consequence. To turn from God is to turn from life. The Babylonian exile wasn't a cosmic tantrum—it was the logical outcome of spiritual adultery.

And yet, even in judgment, mercy spoke louder. Every exile was followed by a promise. "Comfort, comfort My people," Isaiah proclaimed. "Speak tenderly to Jerusalem." God's anger was not the opposite of His love; it was the expression of it. A father disciplines not to destroy but to restore.

Through these centuries, something remarkable was happening: humanity was slowly being taught to recognise a different kind of divinity. The pagan gods demanded sacrifice to earn their favour. The God of Israel offered covenant to share His life. The pagan gods were impersonal and cruel; Israel's God was personal and faithful. The pagan gods needed humans to feed them; Israel's God fed His people with manna from heaven.

The entire drama of the Old Covenant is about re-education—unlearning the lies of idolatry and relearning the truth of relationship. God's people were being taught who He was, who they were, and what love required. They were learning to distinguish between the holy and the profane, the clean and the unclean, not as arbitrary ritual but as moral training. Every law about purity and sacrifice carried a deeper lesson: sin contaminates, and holiness heals.

The Tabernacle, that portable temple in the wilderness, was the visual sermon. At its centre stood the Ark of the Covenant—the sign of God's presence. Around it were curtains and veils, altars and basins, all proclaiming one truth: you cannot simply barge into holiness. Sin has made the world unsafe for glory. But through sacrifice, through priesthood, through atonement, access was made possible again—foreshadowing the day when the veil would finally be torn in two.

The priests themselves were symbols of mediation. Clothed in white linen, anointed with oil, they stood between God and the people, bearing the names of the tribes on their garments as they offered sacrifice. Their role anticipated the true High Priest who would one day enter not into a man-made sanctuary but into heaven itself, bearing the whole world upon His heart.

And the sacrifices—they were not bribes but signposts. Each animal laid upon the altar was a shadow cast backward from Calvary. The blood of bulls and goats could not take away sin, but it could teach humanity that reconciliation costs life. Every Passover lamb, every scapegoat driven into the wilderness, was an acted prophecy of the Lamb of God who would take away the sins of the world.

Thus the Old Covenant was not the problem but the preparation. It was God's patient pedagogy, His divine schooling of a people who had forgotten how to trust. In the Law they learned justice; in the

Prophets they learned mercy; in sacrifice they learned that sin destroys and love restores. The Incarnation would be the moment all those lessons converged.

God had been writing in symbols what He would one day write in flesh.

By the time of the prophets, Israel had learned that God was unlike any of the deities that surrounded them. He was not confined to a temple or a region. He was not bound by seasons or by fate. He was free — utterly, dangerously free — and yet faithful to His promises. This paradox of freedom and fidelity is the heartbeat of the Old Covenant. God cannot be manipulated, but He can be trusted.

The prophets served as both conscience and compass for the nation. When kings forgot the covenant, prophets reminded them that the Law was not merely a national code but a revelation of God's own character. Isaiah, Jeremiah, Ezekiel, and Hosea were not innovators; they were interpreters, translating divine love into human language. And their message, though often fierce, was always rooted in mercy: "Return to Me, and I will return to you."

Take Hosea. God commands him to marry a woman who will betray him, to live through the pain of faithfulness to the unfaithful. The marriage becomes a living parable of God's relationship with Israel. When Hosea buys back his adulterous wife from slavery, God says, "So I will betroth you to Me forever." Through human heartbreak, divine love becomes visible.

Isaiah's prophecies expand this love to cosmic proportions. He speaks not just to Israel but to the nations, announcing a future when God's salvation will reach the ends of the earth. The vision of the suffering servant, "wounded for our transgressions," points to a redemption that will transcend every border and law. The Servant will carry the iniquity of many, offering His life as a ransom for all. Isaiah is already preaching Christ, centuries before Bethlehem.

Jeremiah, the "weeping prophet," reveals another aspect of God's heart — tenderness in the midst of judgment. He speaks of a new covenant, not written on stone but on the human heart. The old Law showed what holiness looked like; the new would infuse holiness from within. Jeremiah's words are the bridge between Sinai and Calvary, between commandment and grace. "I will forgive their iniquity," God promises through him, "and I will remember their sin no more."

Ezekiel takes the vision further still. Amid the ruins of exile, he proclaims a resurrection of hope: dry bones covered with flesh, a dead nation revived by the breath of God. His vision is more than national restoration; it is a prophecy of spiritual rebirth. The Spirit that will one day raise Christ from the dead is already hovering over Ezekiel's valley, whispering of what's to come: "I will put My Spirit within you, and you shall live."

Through these prophets, the tone of revelation shifts. God is no longer simply commanding righteousness from above; He is promising to create righteousness from within. He is preparing humanity for an intimacy that will exceed comprehension — not God over man, not even God beside man, but God within man.

And yet, even as revelation deepens, human resistance remains. Israel's history is an endless cycle of faith and failure, devotion and defiance. The same people who sang at the Red Sea worshipped a golden calf within weeks. The same city that welcomed the ark of the covenant with dancing later filled its temples with idols. Humanity's heart, it seems, is always divided.

But the failure of man never nullifies the faithfulness of God. That is perhaps the most important lesson of the Old Testament. Again and again, when Israel breaks the covenant, God renews it. When they turn from Him, He pursues them. When they fall into exile, He brings them home. His mercy is relentless, His patience inexhaustible.

That relentlessness reveals something crucial: salvation is not humanity's climb to heaven but heaven's descent to humanity. Every act of covenant is another step downward — God stooping lower, speaking clearer, coming closer. He meets Abraham under the stars, Moses in the fire, Elijah in a whisper. He is not waiting for us to find Him; He is moving toward us through history.

By the time the Old Testament closes, humanity has learned two essential truths. First: there is one God, personal and faithful, who acts in history and loves His people not abstractly but passionately. Second: the human heart, though chosen and instructed, cannot keep faith on its own. The Law has revealed the path but not the power.

That tension sets the stage for the Incarnation. The entire Old Covenant is a divine drama designed to teach the world its need — to show that external commandments cannot create internal transformation. The Law could tell us what righteousness is; it could not make us righteous. The prophets could point to the future, but they could not bring it near.

As the centuries passed, Israel's longing deepened. The sacrifices, once vibrant, began to feel like echoes. The prophets' voices grew silent after Malachi. The heavens, it seemed, had closed. The people still gathered in synagogues, still recited the psalms, still waited for deliverance — but the air was heavy with absence. Four hundred years of divine silence stretched between the Testaments, a silence that felt like judgment but was really gestation.

For in that silence, the world was being prepared. The Roman roads were being built, the Greek language spread, the Jewish Scriptures translated. The stage of history was set for a message that would need to travel quickly, understood by many nations. When God finally spoke again, He would speak not in thunder or through stone tablets, but in a child's cry — the Word made flesh.

But before we reach that child, we must understand the full weight of the preparation. The Old Covenant was not failure; it was foundation.

Without it, the Gospel would make no sense. The Law taught holiness; the Prophets taught hope; the Sacrifices taught atonement. Together they formed a grammar of grace, so that when Grace Himself arrived, the world would know how to read Him.

Every commandment, every covenant, every prophet was one more syllable in the long divine sentence that would end with the name *Jesus*.

When we read the Old Testament through this lens, what once seemed strange or severe begins to glow with purpose. Behind every law and lament, every war and wandering, there is a single heartbeat: God refusing to abandon the world He made. His revelation unfolds not in a flash, but like dawn—first dim light, then colour, then the full brightness of day.

Theologians call this the "divine pedagogy": God teaching humanity as a father teaches his children. You cannot explain calculus to a toddler; you begin with numbers and stories. Likewise, God begins with covenants, symbols, and rituals—training the human imagination to recognise holiness. Each command, each feast, each prophet is a lesson in the grammar of grace.

This gradual approach tells us something vital about God's character. He does not impose; He invites. He does not overwhelm; He woos. When the world had forgotten Him, He did not shout from the heavens but whispered through a people. The patience of God in the Old Covenant is almost scandalous. He bears betrayal without abandoning, disobedience without withdrawal. Even His judgments are merciful, for they are meant to awaken, not annihilate.

Consider how often the covenant is renewed despite failure. After the golden calf, God renews it. After the wilderness rebellion, He renews it. After the exile, He renews it again. The thread of mercy is unbreakable. "If we are faithless, He remains faithful," writes Paul, echoing the entire Old Testament story. God's fidelity is not dependent on human performance; it flows from His nature.

This is why the Old Testament is not, as some imagine, a record of divine wrath but of divine restraint. The Creator of the universe, insulted by His creatures, could have ended the story with a word. Instead, He chooses relationship. He stays in the story. His anger, when it appears, is never capricious—it is the wound of rejected love. The prophets often describe His anger in the language of heartbreak: "What more could I have done for My vineyard that I have not done?"

Such divine sorrow reveals a profound truth: God's justice is not the opposite of His love; it is its consequence. Only those who care deeply can be truly angry. Indifference is the absence of love, not its perfection. When God disciplines His people, He does so as a parent disciplines a child—to restore, not to crush. Even His punishments are laced with promise: "For a brief moment I abandoned you, but with great compassion I will gather you."

This interplay of justice and mercy, of holiness and intimacy, defines the Old Covenant. It's what makes the Hebrew Scriptures unlike any other ancient literature. The gods of Mesopotamia or Greece are powerful but capricious. They use humanity as pawns in their celestial dramas. The God of Israel, by contrast, binds Himself to a promise of love—and keeps it even when the other party doesn't. He is both sovereign and self-giving, transcendent and tender.

In that sense, the Old Testament is the world's first revelation of *grace*. It shows a God who chooses before being chosen, who loves before being loved, who forgives before being asked. The covenant with Abraham was unconditional: "I will bless you." The deliverance from Egypt was undeserved: "I have heard your cry." The Law at Sinai was given to those already freed: "I am the Lord your God who brought you out." At every step, grace precedes command.

Even the sacrificial system, often seen as primitive, was an act of mercy. In a world steeped in blood rituals and human sacrifice, God redirected the instinct toward something redemptive. He took a practice of fear and transformed it into a pedagogy of faith. The animals were not food for the gods but symbols of substitution—the innocent bearing the weight of the guilty. They taught that sin is not a private defect but a rupture that requires reconciliation.

But the deeper lesson of sacrifice was this: forgiveness costs. Love that heals must suffer. Every animal on Israel's altars was a whisper of Calvary. The lamb without blemish, the scapegoat driven into the wilderness, the blood sprinkled on the mercy seat—all were previews of the final exchange, when God Himself would become the offering.

Even the architecture of Israel's worship pointed forward. The Tabernacle and later the Temple were not divine real estate but theological blueprints. The outer court, the holy place, and the holy of holies mirrored heaven, earth, and the human heart. At the centre, behind the veil, the Ark of the Covenant held the tablets of the Law—God's word enclosed in wood and gold. One day, that pattern would repeat in a person: the Word enclosed in flesh. The Temple was prophecy in architecture.

And the Ark? It was carried through the wilderness, through water and war, guarded like the heart of the nation. Wherever the Ark went, victory followed, because it was the tangible sign of God's presence. When Mary later carried Christ in her womb and visited Elizabeth, the language Luke uses mirrors the story of the Ark entering the house of Obed-Edom. The old Ark bore the Word written on stone; the new Ark bore the Word made flesh.

All of this shows that the Old Covenant is not a failed attempt replaced by something better. It is the soil from which the Gospel grows. The God who spoke through burning bush and cloud and prophet is the same God who will speak through His Son. The revelation changes form, not substance. The voice that thundered on Sinai will one day whisper in a carpenter's shop.

But even now, centuries before that carpenter is born, God is preparing the world. Israel's monotheism stands alone in a sea of polytheism. Its ethical code, rooted in human dignity, prepares civilisation for moral clarity. Its expectation of a Messiah ignites the human imagination with hope. The entire Old Covenant is a divine apprenticeship in longing.

By the time of the Second Temple, Israel has learned to wait. The prophets have fallen silent, but their words echo in every prayer, every feast, every psalm sung in exile. "How long, O Lord?" becomes the cry of the faithful. The Law has done its work; the people know their need. They have discovered that knowledge of good and evil does not give life. Only the presence of God can do that—and that presence, once veiled in smoke, will soon walk among them.

When the dawn of the Incarnation finally breaks, the light will not appear suddenly. It will rise from the horizon that the Old Covenant has drawn, the long, patient sunrise of revelation.

The great thread that runs through the Old Covenant is one word: *faithfulness.* Humanity keeps breaking promises, and God keeps renewing them. The Hebrew Scriptures are less the story of man seeking God and more the story of God refusing to give up.

The Law, the prophets, and the sacrifices form the threefold cord of that faithfulness. Each reveals a different side of divine persistence: the Law reveals His holiness, the prophets reveal His mercy, and the sacrifices reveal His justice. Together they teach that God's plan is not to abolish creation but to heal it from within.

By the time Israel returned from exile in Babylon, the nation had changed profoundly. Idolatry—the worship of false gods—was gone. Centuries of suffering had purged the people of polytheism. They now understood that there was only one God, the Maker of heaven and earth, who ruled history and judged nations. Monotheism had taken root. But the people also knew, more clearly than ever, that holiness was impossible without grace. They had kept the Law, built the Temple anew, offered sacrifice faithfully, and yet still felt distant from the divine presence.

This sense of incompletion saturates the later books of the Old Testament. The Temple stands again, but the Shekinah—the visible glory that once filled it—does not return. The people are back in the land, yet they remain under foreign empires. They possess the Law, yet long for liberation. The covenant feels unfinished, like a melody awaiting resolution.

That waiting becomes the defining posture of Israel. The prophets have promised a Messiah—a king from David's line who will rule with justice and restore the covenant forever. The people wait through centuries of occupation, oppression, and silence. The Psalms begin to sound like prayers not of triumph but of endurance: "Out of the depths I cry to You, O Lord."

It is in this silence that faith matures. The absence of revelation does not mean abandonment; it means gestation. Like the seed buried in the soil, the Word is preparing to sprout. The centuries between Malachi and Matthew are the womb of salvation history.

During this time, Jewish thought deepens. The idea of resurrection emerges more clearly. Hope shifts from earthly prosperity to eternal life. The prophets' promise of a new heart begins to be understood as something supernatural. Wisdom literature like *Proverbs*, *Sirach*, and *Wisdom of Solomon* reflects on the mystery of divine justice and the problem of death. God is training His people to long not for worldly triumph but for union with Him beyond the grave.

Meanwhile, through the spread of the Greek and Roman empires, the world itself is being prepared. Roads and trade routes connect lands that were once isolated. Greek becomes a common language, capable of carrying ideas across cultures. Philosophy refines the human hunger for meaning. Rome, with its legal order and infrastructure, unwittingly builds the skeleton on which the Gospel will travel. The stage of history is set for the universal message of Christ.

In all this, the invisible hand of God is at work. The same God who guided Abraham under the stars now guides empires and philosophers toward the fullness of time. The divine pedagogy extends beyond Israel to the world: the Law and prophets prepare the chosen people, while reason and philosophy prepare the nations. The Incarnation will unite both—the faith of Israel and the search for truth in Greece and Rome—into one revelation.

But before we reach that moment, it's important to understand why the Old Covenant had to exist at all. Could not God have simply sent His Son immediately after the Fall? Why centuries of law, blood, and prophecy?

The answer lies in the nature of relationship. Love that is imposed is not love. God wanted not slaves but sons, not puppets but partners. To prepare humanity for divine union, He had to cultivate freedom. The Law was a tutor, teaching us moral order. The prophets were counsellors, awakening conscience. The sacrifices were reminders of sin's cost. Through all of it, God was forming a people capable of recognising Him when He came—not as a tyrant but as a bridegroom.

The covenants, then, are not divine bureaucracy; they are divine courtship. The Creator pursues His creation like a lover seeking the heart of the beloved. Each covenant is a proposal of love, escalating in intimacy. With Noah, God promises never to destroy. With Abraham, He promises to bless. With Moses, He binds Himself in law. With David, He pledges eternal kingship. And with Christ, He will consummate the union in blood—the marriage of heaven and earth.

The prophets understood this spousal symbolism well. Hosea speaks of God as a faithful husband and Israel as an unfaithful bride. Ezekiel describes the covenant as God clothing, adorning, and cherishing His beloved. Isaiah proclaims, "Your Maker is your husband, the Lord of hosts is His name." These are not metaphors of sentiment but of covenant reality. God's faithfulness is marital; it is total and self-giving.

This is why idolatry is described as adultery. It is not merely wrong belief but broken relationship. To worship idols is to cheat on the One who made you. And yet, astonishingly, every time Israel betrays Him, God forgives. He disciplines but does not divorce. His love is covenantal—bound not by feeling but by promise.

That pattern prepares us for the Cross. What begins in the faithlessness of Israel ends in the faithfulness of Christ. Humanity's "no" will be answered by God's final "yes." The covenant that man keeps breaking will finally be kept from both sides—by the God who becomes man.

The Old Covenant, therefore, is not obsolete history; it is divine autobiography. It reveals who God is: a lover who commits, forgives, and stays. The Incarnation will not replace this story but fulfill it. The God who once spoke from fire will soon walk in flesh, bearing in His heart all the promises ever made.

In Him, the covenant will cease to be written on stone or scrolls; it will be written in blood.

When we look at the Old Covenant as a single unfolding story, a pattern begins to emerge. Every generation of Israel repeats the same rhythm: revelation, rebellion, repentance, renewal. It is the heartbeat of divine pedagogy. God speaks, man strays, God restores. Far from being repetitive, this rhythm teaches us something fundamental about both human nature and divine patience.

Humanity learns slowly. We forget quickly. God, by contrast, is endlessly patient. Each covenant cycle draws humanity a little closer to understanding that the heart of the Law is not rule but relationship. "I will be your God, and you will be My people" — that refrain echoes across centuries. It is not merely a contract of obedience; it is an invitation to communion.

Consider the period of the Judges. Israel, now settled in the Promised

Land, quickly falls into complacency. They forget the God who freed them and turn again to idols. Oppression follows, then repentance, then deliverance. Each judge — Gideon, Samson, Deborah, Samuel — prefigures a future Redeemer who will free not from political tyranny but from spiritual slavery. The lesson is clear: every earthly saviour fails because the real enemy is within. The problem is not the nations around Israel but the rebellion within Israel's heart.

Then come the kings. The people demand a monarch "like the nations." God grants their wish, and through their desire, He weaves redemption. Saul shows the danger of pride, David the beauty of repentance, Solomon the tragedy of idolatry cloaked in wisdom. In each figure, we see glimmers and distortions of the true King to come. David's psalms, especially, reveal the soul's anatomy before God — sin confessed, mercy received, covenant renewed. "Create in me a clean heart, O God," he prays, and the cry becomes the anthem of all fallen humanity.

The Davidic covenant marks a turning point. God promises that David's throne will endure forever. Centuries later, when empires rise and Israel's monarchy collapses, that promise becomes the backbone of hope. The Messiah — the Anointed One — will come from David's line. He will unite the roles of king, priest, and prophet. He will rule not only Israel but all nations.

Through this promise, the meaning of covenant deepens again. It's no longer just about a people; it's about a person. The covenant begins to take shape around an individual figure who embodies Israel itself — the righteous servant, the faithful son. In the Psalms and prophets, the identity of this figure becomes more distinct: a suffering king who will reign through sacrifice. The seed of the woman who will crush the serpent's head; the Son of David whose throne will never end; the servant who will bear the sins of many — all point toward one reality.

At this stage, revelation becomes increasingly moral and interior.

The prophets shift the focus from ritual to righteousness, from sacrifice to sincerity. Amos thunders, "Let justice roll down like waters." Isaiah calls fasting useless without compassion. Jeremiah insists that circumcision must be of the heart, not merely the flesh. The old external signs remain, but they are now seen as training wheels for the inner life.

This is not evolution from primitive to sophisticated religion — it is revelation moving from shadow to substance. God is preparing humanity for the moment when the Law will no longer be written on tablets of stone but on hearts of flesh. Each prophet adds another brushstroke to the portrait of grace.

Yet Israel resists this interiorisation. External religion is easier than internal conversion. It's safer to perform rituals than to surrender the heart. So the people cling to the forms of faith while ignoring its spirit. They bring sacrifices but neglect justice. They pray in the temple but exploit the poor. The prophets, weary yet relentless, expose the hypocrisy. "Your hands are full of blood," Isaiah cries. "Wash yourselves; make yourselves clean."

The exile that follows — first to Assyria, then Babylon — is both punishment and purification. Cut off from their land, temple, and sacrifices, Israel is forced to ask what faith means without these external supports. And there, in foreign soil, the deepest truths of revelation ripen. The Psalms of exile speak of longing not for possessions but for presence: "By the rivers of Babylon we sat and wept when we remembered Zion."

In exile, the Word of God moves inward. The synagogue replaces the temple; Scripture replaces sacrifice. Faith becomes portable. Prayer, fasting, and almsgiving — the spiritual disciplines later sanctified by Christ — take root here. The Law becomes not just national identity but personal devotion. The idea of holiness shifts from ritual purity to moral fidelity. The people begin to grasp that true worship is obedience of the heart.

This purification prepares the ground for the final covenant. The prophets foresee it but cannot yet name it. "Behold, the days are coming," Jeremiah says, "when I will make a new covenant." Ezekiel echoes: "I will sprinkle clean water upon you, and you shall be clean. I will give you a new heart and put My Spirit within you." Hosea promises that this covenant will be like marriage restored after infidelity. Isaiah prophesies that it will be sealed not in ink or law but in suffering: "By His stripes we are healed."

Thus, by the time the Old Testament closes, two truths have crystallised in the collective conscience of Israel: first, that God is perfectly faithful; second, that humanity cannot be faithful without divine help. The Law has revealed sin; the prophets have revealed grace; the sacrifices have revealed the cost. What remains is for God Himself to step into the covenant and fulfill it from both sides.

When the Word becomes flesh, He will not abolish the old patterns; He will inhabit them. He will be the Law fulfilled, the Prophet who speaks life, the Priest who offers Himself, the King who reigns through love. The long preparation of the Old Covenant will find its answer not in a new religion but in a Person.

That Person is already foreshadowed in every page of the Hebrew Scriptures. He is the seed promised to Eve, the ram provided to Abraham, the manna in the wilderness, the water from the rock, the glory that fills the temple, the voice in the burning bush. Every thread of revelation converges in Him.

The Old Covenant ends not with failure but with expectation — a held breath, a pause before the symphony's final movement. History has been tuned to receive the melody that will resolve every dissonance.

And then, one quiet night, in a backwater village under foreign rule, the Word that once thundered from Sinai will cry in the arms of His mother.

The culmination of the Old Covenant comes not in triumph but in yearning. Israel's history closes with longing, not resolution. The prophets have spoken, the psalms have been sung, the temple has been rebuilt—but the people still wait. They are waiting for what the Law promised but could not deliver, for what the prophets foresaw but could not accomplish.

The Law had formed a nation; now the world awaited a Saviour. The centuries between Malachi and the Gospels are known as the "intertestamental period," but spiritually they are a furnace of preparation. Outwardly, the world was moving under Rome's shadow; inwardly, the human soul was aching for redemption.

The silence of God in those years was not absence but anticipation. Like a composer holding a final note before the crescendo, God's quiet was filled with meaning. His people were ready for fulfillment, and the world beyond Israel—educated by Greek reason and Roman order—was ready to hear a universal message.

At this moment in history, every human longing seemed to converge. The Greeks had asked the great questions—What is truth? What is the good? What is happiness?—but found no final answer. The Romans had built a civilisation of law and order, but their hearts remained empty. The Jews carried revelation, but they knew it was incomplete. The stage of humanity was perfectly set for God to enter His own play.

Yet before the curtain rises on the Incarnation, it is worth looking once more at the patterns God wove in Israel's story, because they reveal the logic of what He is about to do.

The Old Covenant was structured around three interlocking realities: covenant, priesthood, and sacrifice. Every one of these was preparation for Christ.

First, covenant.

In the ancient world, covenants were not mere agreements; they were bonds of kinship. Two parties became family by oath and blood.

By binding Himself to humanity through covenant, God wasn't making a deal; He was making adoption possible. With Noah, He promised to preserve life; with Abraham, to bless the nations; with Moses, to sanctify His people; with David, to give an eternal King. Each covenant drew humanity deeper into divine intimacy. And each one ended the same way—human unfaithfulness met by divine fidelity.

In Jesus, God will enter the covenant not as the partner but as the participant. He will fulfill both sides—man's obedience and God's promise. On the Cross, divine and human faithfulness will finally meet.

Second, priesthood.

From the beginning, the priest's role was mediation: standing between God and man, offering sacrifice for sin, and blessing the people. The priest symbolised humanity's longing to be reconciled. But no priest could bridge the chasm completely, because he was as fallen as those he served. His sacrifices, therefore, had to be repeated endlessly.

The Levitical priesthood was a shadow pointing toward a greater reality. When Christ comes, He will be both priest and victim—the one who offers and the one who is offered. The priesthood of Aaron was a rehearsal; the priesthood of Christ will be reality. "You are a priest forever," says the psalmist, "after the order of Melchizedek." That mysterious priest-king who blessed Abraham with bread and wine foreshadows the Eucharist—the new sacrifice of the new covenant.

Third, sacrifice.

If covenant is relationship and priesthood is mediation, sacrifice is love in action. In every culture, sacrifice expressed the same truth: something precious must be given to restore what has been broken. But Israel's sacrifices differed from pagan ones in two crucial ways. First, they were commanded by God, not invented by man. Second, they were never final. The blood of lambs and bulls could cover sin symbolically but not cleanse it completely. The sacrifices were reminders of guilt, not removers of it.

Still, they trained the human heart to understand the cost of redemption. Every time an animal was laid on the altar, Israel was being tutored in the grammar of atonement: life for life, blood for blood, love for love. When the true Lamb of God came, they would recognise the language.

And so the Law, the priesthood, and the sacrifices—though temporary—formed the divine vocabulary by which humanity could one day comprehend Calvary.

This is why Christianity cannot be understood apart from Judaism. The Old Testament is not a failed attempt at religion; it is revelation in progress. God was writing a story too vast to be told in one act. The first half is promise; the second half is fulfillment. Together they form one drama, one Word, one covenant.

For the early Church, this continuity was self-evident. The apostles preached Christ not as the rejection of the Law but as its completion. "Do not think that I have come to abolish the Law or the Prophets," Jesus would say, "but to fulfill them." Fulfillment, not replacement—that is the logic of grace.

To see how profound this fulfillment is, imagine reading a mystery novel where every clue, every shadow, every conversation suddenly clicks into place at the final page. The Old Testament is that web of clues. The Exodus anticipates baptism; the manna anticipates the Eucharist; the temple anticipates the Incarnation; the Passover anticipates the Passion. Even Israel's failures—her idolatries, her exiles—anticipate the Cross, where God will bear in Himself the rebellion of His people and turn it into redemption.

Nothing in Israel's story is wasted. Every triumph and tragedy, every psalm and prophecy, is a thread in the tapestry of salvation. When Christ comes, He will not tear it apart; He will turn it over to show the image that was hidden in the weaving.

The Old Covenant, then, is not ancient history. It is the anatomy of grace. It shows us what it means to be chosen, to be loved, to be formed, to fail, and to be forgiven. It teaches us that God's answer to human rebellion is always relationship. When we walk away, He follows. When we sin, He disciplines. When we return, He rejoices.

This pattern—of mercy without compromise, of justice married to love—is the heartbeat of Scripture. It is also the reason why the Incarnation is not an accident of history but its destiny. God's descent into flesh is the natural conclusion of a covenant that has always been about presence.

In the Old Covenant, He walked with Abraham, thundered to Moses, whispered to Elijah, dwelt in the temple. In the New Covenant, He will dwell in human nature itself. The divine patience that endured centuries of failure will at last take form in a person, visible, touchable, crucifiable.

The story of Israel is the story of how God made that possible—by teaching humanity, step by step, that holiness is not a code but a communion, and that love, to be real, must take on flesh.

The Old Covenant ends where the New begins: at the threshold of expectation. Centuries of revelation have narrowed to a single point of focus—a promise waiting to be fulfilled. The Law has done its work, exposing sin and defining righteousness. The prophets have done theirs, stirring hope and pointing forward. The sacrifices have kept alive the understanding that sin demands atonement and that blood must somehow heal what is broken.

Everything in Israel's story has prepared the world for one truth: humanity cannot climb to God; God must descend to humanity. The tower of Babel fell because man tried to reach heaven by human effort. The covenant endures because God keeps coming down. From the rainbow after the flood to the fire on Sinai, revelation has always been divine initiative. The Incarnation will be the final descent—the Word stooping to the dust He once shaped.

When that Word finally comes, it will not arrive in majesty but in humility. The long history of Israel has proven that power does not save hearts; only love does. So when God takes flesh, He will not appear in the palace of a king but in the womb of a virgin. The same God who once wrote His Law on stone will now inscribe His mercy on skin.

Mary's "yes" to the angel becomes the hinge of history. In her, the story of Israel reaches its climax: she is the daughter of Zion, the ark of the covenant, the living temple. Everything that the Old Covenant symbolised is now fulfilled in her consent. The Word that spoke creation into being enters creation through her faith. The God who dwelt behind the veil of the Temple now takes up residence in her womb.

With that moment, the centuries of silence break. The God who once thundered to Moses now coos as an infant. The divine fire that descended on Sinai now flickers as candlelight in a Bethlehem stable. The One who wrote commandments now learns to hold a carpenter's hand.

The Old Covenant had taught humanity to expect holiness as distance: the holy mountain fenced off, the holy of holies entered only by a priest, the divine name too sacred to utter. Now, in Christ, holiness becomes proximity. The untouchable God can be held. The invisible God has a face. The ineffable God speaks with human words. The Lawgiver walks among lawbreakers not to condemn but to call them friends.

The Incarnation does not erase the old story; it fulfils every line of it. The Word made flesh is the living synthesis of all God's dealings with man. The covenant with Noah preserved creation; in Christ, creation is renewed. The promise to Abraham that all nations would be blessed finds its completion in a Messiah who dies for every nation. The Law of Moses, which could only diagnose sin, finds its cure in the blood of the new Passover Lamb. The throne of David, long empty, is filled by the Son whose reign will have no end.

What began as law becomes life; what began as promise becomes presence. The divine patience of millennia condenses into one heartbeat in the chest of a child.

When Jesus begins His ministry, He does not discard Israel's faith; He perfects it. His Sermon on the Mount does not contradict Moses but completes him: "You have heard it said… but I say to you." Each "but I say" is the voice of the same God who once said, "I am." The continuity is breathtaking. The voice on Sinai now speaks from a hillside in Galilee. The fire that once burned on the mountain now burns in a human heart.

This is why the Incarnation is not an interruption in history but its fulfilment. The God who has always desired to dwell with His people finally does so in the most intimate way possible. In the wilderness, His presence rested on the Ark; in Mary, it rests in the flesh. In the temple, His glory filled a room; in Jesus, it fills a human life. The divine name, once unspoken, now has a human syllable: *Jesus*—YHWH saves.

The Old Covenant has reached its destination. All the symbols, shadows, and sacrifices have met their reality. The commandments that once hung over humanity as accusation are now embodied as mercy. The priesthood that once mediated from afar now kneels beside the sinner. The God who once demanded sacrifice now becomes the sacrifice.

When John the Baptist looks at Jesus and declares, "Behold, the Lamb of God who takes away the sin of the world," he is not inventing new theology; he is naming the end of the old. The lambs of Israel pointed toward this moment. The blood that once protected the firstborn in Egypt now redeems the whole world. The Passover that freed slaves from Pharaoh now frees souls from death.

At that instant, all of salvation history converges. Every covenant finds its seal, every prophecy its fulfilment, every longing its home. The God of Abraham, Isaac, and Jacob has kept His promise—not by sending a message, but by coming Himself.

The Old Covenant was a school of longing. Its laws taught humanity's need for holiness; its failures taught the need for grace; its sacrifices taught the cost of forgiveness. Through it, God revealed not only His justice but His mercy, not only His transcendence but His tenderness. And when the fullness of time came, He stepped into His own lesson, embodying the truths He had taught.

That is the meaning of the Incarnation: God did not change His plan; He completed it. The Old Covenant was always meant to lead here—to a Person who would embody all its promises and exceed all its expectations.

If the story of the Old Testament is God saying, "I will come to you," then the story of the New is Him saying, "I am here."

The child in the manger is not the beginning of a new religion but the continuation of the oldest relationship in the world: the Creator's relentless pursuit of His creatures. In Him, the Law becomes love, the command becomes communion, and the promise becomes presence.

The long preparation of Israel teaches us what kind of God we serve—one who keeps His word even when we break ours. The Old Covenant is proof that divine patience is not weakness but power, and that love, to be perfect, must wait until it can give itself completely.

And now, having descended through covenants and centuries, that love stands ready to do what no law, prophet, or sacrifice ever could: to save not just a people but all people; not just a nation but the world.

3

The Incarnation: When God Stepped In

If there is a single hinge on which the entire Christian faith turns, it is the Incarnation — the claim that the eternal God became man. Strip that away, and Christianity collapses into moral philosophy, a system of ethics no more binding than any other. Keep it, and everything else follows: the Cross, the Resurrection, the sacraments, the hope of heaven. The Incarnation is not an ornament on the faith; it is the engine.

But what does it actually mean? Not in the abstract language of theology, but in the simple, concrete sense of the claim itself: that the Creator of the universe, infinite and eternal, stepped into His own creation and took on flesh. That the Author wrote Himself into the story. That the Maker of galaxies nursed at a woman's breast, stumbled as a child, worked with calloused hands, and one day hung on wood He had once formed.

This is the most staggering idea in history. It is either madness or truth; there is no middle ground. Every other religion has prophets, sages, and mystics—men who reach toward God. Christianity begins with God reaching toward man, not by word or symbol but by presence.

The Incarnation answers a question older than time: *Can the infinite touch the finite without destroying it?* The Old Covenant taught us to fear that contact—mountains shaking, temples trembling, mortals forbidden to look upon glory and live. But in Bethlehem, the unapproachable light wraps itself in humility. The fire that once burned on Sinai now flickers as the light of an infant's eyes. The uncontainable God makes Himself containable, not by ceasing to be God, but by choosing to dwell within the limits He created.

To understand why He did this, we must return to the wound that made it necessary. Humanity's separation from God is not a surface problem. It's not ignorance to be corrected, nor behaviour to be improved. It is a rupture in being itself. When the first humans turned from God, they turned from the very source of life. The result was not simply guilt but death. We didn't just lose paradise; we lost participation in divine life.

Every religion since has been an attempt, in one form or another, to climb back. Sacrifice, law, meditation, moral striving—all are variations of the same instinct: to restore what was lost. But none can succeed, because the gap is infinite. Finite creatures cannot bridge an infinite divide. If the problem were ignorance, God could have sent more teachers. If the problem were behaviour, He could have sent better laws. But the problem is death, and the only remedy for death is life itself.

That is why God did not send advice or improvement, but Himself. Saint Athanasius, one of the earliest defenders of this mystery, said it plainly: "The Word became man so that man might become god." He didn't mean that humanity becomes divine by nature, but that by union with the divine life we share in its power and immortality. The Incarnation is the meeting point of two worlds—the eternal and the temporal, heaven and earth, Creator and creature.

Imagine a deep chasm separating a cliff of light from a canyon of darkness. No bridge built from the dark side can reach the other, for the materials themselves are corrupt. The only way across is if the light extends itself, laying down beams from its side until they span the gap. That is the Incarnation: God extending Himself into creation, forming the bridge from His side.

This is why Christianity insists that salvation cannot come from man. Every human religion begins from the ground up. The Gospel begins from the sky down. The Son of God doesn't stand at the edge calling for us to jump; He comes down, takes our hand, and lifts us up.

The logic of it is as breathtaking as its mercy. If sin separated God and man, reconciliation requires one who is both. Saint Anselm put it in his famous question, *Cur Deus Homo?* — "Why did God become man?" His answer was simple and airtight: the debt of sin was owed by man, but only God could pay it. Therefore, the Redeemer must be both God and man. Only the divine could offer an infinite act of love to heal an infinite offense, and only a human could offer it on behalf of humanity.

This dual necessity is not a poetic flourish; it's metaphysical reality. God did not become man because He needed to experience what it's like to suffer. He became man because only in that union could justice and mercy meet. Without justice, mercy would be indulgence. Without mercy, justice would be annihilation. In Christ, both are fulfilled.

The Church calls this union of divine and human natures in the one person of Christ the *hypostatic union*. It sounds technical, but its meaning is simple: in Jesus, God and man are joined without confusion, change, division, or separation. He is not half God and half man, but fully both. His divinity is not diminished by His humanity, nor His humanity dissolved by His divinity. Heaven and earth meet in one consciousness, one will, one heart.

Think of iron placed in fire. The metal remains metal, but it takes on the properties of fire—heat and light. So the humanity of Christ remains human, yet it glows with the fire of divinity. When He touches the leper, it is human flesh that touches, but divine power that heals. When He weeps at Lazarus's tomb, His sorrow is real, but within those tears beats the heart of God.

This is not myth. It's mechanics—divinity entering mortality to restore what mortality cannot fix. If you imagine a doctor curing the world's deadliest disease, you glimpse a fraction of the logic. Humanity is terminal, infected by sin. To heal it, the Physician must take the sickness into Himself. The Incarnation is that act—the beginning of the cure.

But it is more than a remedy; it is revelation. For the first time, humanity sees what God is truly like, not through symbols or voices but through a face. "He who has seen Me has seen the Father," Jesus will say. The Incarnation is God's self-portrait. Every healing, every parable, every gesture of Christ is a translation of divine love into human form.

Before this, people could imagine God's power. They could sense His majesty in thunder and sea. But they could not conceive His tenderness. In Christ, the infinite becomes intimate. God is not just the source of life but the friend of sinners, the shepherd searching for lost sheep, the Father who runs to meet the prodigal.

The Incarnation reveals that divine love is not distant or abstract. It stoops. It kneels. It enters the dirt and danger of the human story. It eats with the unclean, touches the contagious, and forgives the condemned. It is love that refuses to remain theoretical.

And here lies the deepest contrast between Christianity and every other creed. The world's religions tell us what we must do to reach God. The Gospel tells us what God has done to reach us. All others begin with man climbing; this one begins with God descending. All others say, "Earn your way." Christ says, "It is finished."

The Incarnation, then, is not one theological curiosity among others. It is the cornerstone. Without it, the Cross is cruelty, the Resurrection illusion, and heaven a fantasy. But with it, everything holds. For if God has truly entered human flesh, then every act of that flesh carries eternal weight. The blood shed on the Cross is not merely human blood; it is the blood of God.

And that changes everything.

When God became man, He didn't simply appear human; He became human in every sense except sin. The Word didn't wear a disguise. He didn't borrow a body as one might borrow a tool. He took our nature completely—soul, mind, flesh, and will—and united it to His divinity forever. The Incarnation was not a temporary mission; it was a permanent marriage. The divine Son didn't visit humanity; He married it.

This is what Saint John meant when he wrote, "The Word became flesh and dwelt among us." The Greek word for "dwelt" is *eskēnōsen*—literally, "pitched His tent." It recalls the Tabernacle of the Old Covenant, that mysterious tent where God's presence once dwelt among the Israelites. Now the true and final Tabernacle has come: the very body of Christ. The glory that once filled a tent now fills a person.

This idea was so daring that even some early Christians struggled to accept it. The Greeks had been trained to think that divinity and flesh could never meet—that the body was too lowly, too corrupt, too finite. But the Gospel upended their philosophy. In Christ, God declares that the human body is not a prison but a temple, not an obstacle to grace but its vessel. Salvation, therefore, is not an escape from the physical but its transfiguration.

The Incarnation restores the dignity of matter. The world is not a mistake to be fled but a creation to be redeemed. Every human face becomes a reflection of the face God chose to wear. Every act of compassion becomes a participation in divine mercy. The material and the spiritual are reconciled. Heaven and earth shake hands in a carpenter's home.

This union also reveals the heart of divine humility. If you want to understand what God is like, don't start with His power—start with His willingness to stoop. The Almighty chooses the form of a servant. The Infinite becomes an infant. The Creator depends on His creatures for food and shelter. The very One who flung the stars into space learns to walk under them.

No philosopher could have invented such a story. Every human myth that tries to bridge the divine and human does so through disguise—Zeus turning into a bull, Vishnu appearing as an avatar. But these are masks, temporary appearances. In Christianity, God doesn't pretend. He participates. The divine nature and the human nature are united in one Person forever. The Son of God becomes the Son of Man so that the sons of men might become sons of God.

Why did He have to do it this way? Why not simply forgive from afar? Because forgiveness without justice is fiction, and justice without incarnation is impossible. Sin is not a bureaucratic error that can be erased by decree; it is a wound in the fabric of creation, a tear that runs through the heart of humanity itself. To heal it, the Healer must enter the wound.

If sin had been merely intellectual error, a word of correction would suffice. If it were ignorance, a prophet could fix it. But sin is death—the separation of soul from God. And death cannot be repaired from a distance. It must be entered, confronted, and reversed. God could no more forgive sin without incarnation than a surgeon could heal a patient without touching the wound.

That is why the Incarnation is not merely a moral example; it is metaphysical necessity. It is the only way divine justice and mercy can coexist. The One who is offended becomes the One who makes atonement. The Judge steps down from His bench, takes off His robes, and accepts the sentence Himself.

This is the mystery and beauty of Christianity: that God does not ask humanity to satisfy His justice but satisfies it Himself. Every other religion offers man's attempt to reach God; the Gospel is God's attempt to reach man. Every other creed ends with "do this and live." The Gospel begins with "it is finished."

The Church Fathers called this the "admirable exchange." Humanity gives God mortality; God gives humanity immortality. We offer Him our weakness; He offers us His strength. We bring our sin; He gives His righteousness. "He became what we are," wrote Irenaeus, "that He might make us what He is."

But this exchange does not happen automatically. It happens through union. Just as a branch must be grafted into the vine to share its life, humanity must be united to Christ to share His divinity. The Incarnation makes that union possible. The divine and human are joined in Him so that, through Him, we might be joined to God.

This is why Jesus is not simply a messenger of salvation but salvation itself. His Person *is* the reconciliation. The Cross is not a separate event tacked onto the Incarnation—it is the consummation of it. God took flesh precisely so that He could offer it. The manger points to the mountain. The wood of the cradle foreshadows the wood of the Cross.

When Christ is born, heaven and earth embrace for the first time since Eden. Angels and shepherds, heaven's choirs and earth's poorest, gather at the same altar. The universe bends around this child, because He is the axis on which it turns. "Emmanuel," the prophets had named Him—"God with us." It's not poetic exaggeration. It's literal fact.

From that moment, the world is changed forever. God's presence is no longer limited to holy mountains or hidden temples. He walks its roads. He breathes its air. He sanctifies ordinary things—bread, water, touch, time itself. What had been lost in the Fall is now restored in a deeper form: not merely God above us, not only God around us, but

God within us.

Every act of Christ reveals this divine nearness. When He heals, divinity flows through humanity. When He teaches, eternal wisdom speaks through a human voice. When He weeps, the compassion of God finds expression in human tears. Nothing in His humanity hides His divinity; everything in His humanity reveals it.

And yet, the paradox remains breathtaking. The one who sustains the cosmos learns carpentry from Joseph. The one who upholds the stars sleeps under them. The one who commands the winds endures desert hunger and thirst. Each of these moments is theology in motion—divine power hidden in weakness, omnipotence disguised as vulnerability.

This is what Saint Paul meant when he wrote, "Though He was in the form of God, He did not count equality with God a thing to be grasped, but emptied Himself, taking the form of a servant." This "emptying"—the Greek word *kenosis*—does not mean God ceased to be God. It means He chose not to use His divinity as protection from suffering. Love restrained omnipotence for the sake of mercy.

God's humility is His glory. In becoming man, He revealed not less of Himself but more. The humility of Christ is not divine disguise; it is divine disclosure. Only love powerful enough to make itself small could save a world swollen with pride.

The Incarnation, then, is the paradox that defines Christianity: infinite majesty and total humility united in one person. The God who spoke worlds into being now speaks with a Galilean accent. The one who commands legions of angels allows Himself to be carried in human arms. He does not cease to be infinite, yet He enters finitude fully.

That paradox is not contradiction but revelation. In Christ, we discover that the true nature of divine power is not domination but love—the kind of love that gives, risks, and suffers. The Incarnation reveals that omnipotence is not God's ability to do everything, but His willingness to become small for the sake of others. The Creator stoops not because He must, but because His nature is love, and love always descends.

This is why the Incarnation was not only necessary for our salvation, but also the only way God could fully reveal Himself. The prophets saw glimpses of His holiness, the psalmists felt His mercy, the philosophers inferred His reason. But only in Jesus does the invisible God become visible. "In Him," writes Paul, "the whole fullness of deity dwells bodily." Not symbolically, not partially—bodily.

Think of what that means. The divine and human are no longer parallel lines that never meet; they intersect in a living person. The chasm between Creator and creation is closed, not by human ascent but by divine descent. Heaven and earth are no longer separate realms but interwoven realities, joined forever in the body of Christ.

And because God has taken flesh, every part of human life becomes potential ground for holiness. Work, rest, friendship, sorrow—none of it is beneath God now. When the Word became flesh, He didn't simply touch humanity; He touched everything human. He redeemed labour by working with His hands, family life by living in one, and suffering by enduring it to the end. There is now no corner of existence where God cannot be found.

This is the most radical consequence of the Incarnation: there is no such thing as ordinary life anymore. If God has entered history, then every moment of history carries eternal weight. Every act of kindness can become a participation in divine love; every wound can become a place of encounter with the Crucified. The Incarnation sanctifies existence itself.

Yet to grasp this, we have to understand what the Incarnation is *not*. It is not God pretending to be human, nor is it humanity elevated to divinity by its own effort. It is God truly becoming man, while remaining truly God. Two complete natures—divine and human—united in one person.

The early Church spent centuries defending this truth because it is the linchpin of salvation. Deny Christ's divinity, and you lose redemption; deny His humanity, and you lose identification. If He is not God, He cannot save us. If He is not man, He cannot represent us. The mystery of salvation rests on this balance.

Some early thinkers stumbled at this. The Gnostics, influenced by Greek disdain for matter, claimed that Christ only appeared to have a body—that His flesh was an illusion. But if His body was an illusion, then so was His death, and so is our salvation. Others, like the Arians, insisted that the Son was a creature, exalted but not divine. But if He is not divine, His sacrifice cannot reconcile humanity to God. The Church's response, crystallised at the Councils of Nicaea and Chalcedon, was unambiguous: the one born of Mary is fully God and fully man, consubstantial with the Father according to His divinity, and consubstantial with us according to His humanity.

That language may sound technical, but it protects the simplicity of the Gospel. Without the hypostatic union, Christianity would unravel. The Incarnation is not an optional article of faith; it is the architecture of salvation itself.

Why? Because redemption had to happen from within humanity. The problem of sin is not external to us; it is in our very nature. Therefore, the solution must also enter that nature. As Gregory Nazianzen wrote, "What is not assumed is not healed." In other words, God had to take on every aspect of our humanity to redeem it completely. He took a human mind to heal our ignorance, a human will to heal our disobedience, a human body to heal our corruption, and a human heart to heal our lovelessness. Nothing was left out, because nothing was beyond His mercy.

Here, the logic of divine love becomes luminous. God does not save us from the outside by waving a celestial wand. He saves us from within by joining Himself to what He made. The Incarnation is the slow undoing of death from the inside out.

Think of a poisoned well that infects every drop drawn from it. The only way to cleanse it is to pour in a purer stream. That's what happens in the Incarnation: the pure life of God is poured into the polluted well of human nature, cleansing it at its source.

This is also why Jesus must live an ordinary human life, not just appear at thirty to die on the Cross. His entire existence—childhood, work, friendships, joys, sorrows—is redemptive. Every moment of it infuses divine life into humanity. When He obeys His parents, He redeems family life. When He works with wood, He redeems human labour. When He eats and drinks, He blesses our sustenance. The whole of His life is a sacrament—an outward sign of inward grace.

The Incarnation also changes the meaning of suffering. Before Christ, pain seemed like punishment or meaningless chaos. In Him, it becomes the raw material of redemption. The Son of God did not avoid sorrow; He embraced it. He experienced hunger, fatigue, misunderstanding, betrayal, and death—all the things that make life difficult for us. But by entering them, He transformed them. Suffering, joined to His, becomes salvific. Death, touched by His divinity, becomes the doorway to life.

The mystery goes even deeper. The Incarnation is not just about what God does for us, but what He reveals about us. If God can dwell in human flesh, then human flesh must be capable of God. The Church calls this *capax Dei*—the capacity for God. It means that being human, at its fullest, is not limitation but invitation. We were made for divine communion, and in Christ that possibility is restored.

This changes how we see ourselves and others. The image of God, tarnished by sin, shines again in Christ. To see Him is to see what humanity was always meant to be: radiant with obedience, luminous with love, utterly transparent to the Father's will.

Thus, the Incarnation is not simply God coming to rescue sinners; it is God showing us who we are. The divine Word does not only heal human nature; He reveals its destiny—to share in the very life of God. As Athanasius wrote, "He became man that we might become divine." Not divine by nature, but by participation—the way iron, placed in fire, glows with the fire's heat.

To be Christian, then, is not merely to believe that God once walked among us. It is to live as those in whom He continues to dwell. The Incarnation did not end at the Ascension. The Word made flesh remains forever united to humanity. Heaven now has a human face.

When Christ ascended into heaven, He did not shed His humanity like a costume. He carried it with Him. That is perhaps the most astonishing truth of all: there is now a human body seated at the right hand of the Father. The Incarnation was not a temporary intervention; it is eternal. God did not "try on" humanity for thirty-three years and then return to His former state. He wedded Himself to our nature forever.

That permanence reveals something about God's intention from the beginning. The Incarnation was not a backup plan. It was not Plan B after the Fall. From all eternity, God willed to unite Himself with His creation in love. The sin of Adam made that union necessary for salvation, but not its cause. Even had there been no sin, God would still have entered creation—because divine love always seeks union with what it loves. As the Eastern Fathers put it: "God became man that man might become god." This is not arrogance; it is destiny.

By assuming human nature, the Son of God lifts all of creation into communion with the divine. In Him, matter itself becomes a meeting place between heaven and earth. Bread and wine will one day carry His presence; water will cleanse in baptism; oil will heal the sick. The same world that once hid God's face now becomes the very means by which we encounter Him.

This is why Christianity is unashamedly material. It does not despise the body, the senses, or the world. It blesses them. The sacraments, those visible signs of invisible grace, flow directly from the logic of the Incarnation. Because God has entered matter, matter can now convey God. Because He has taken flesh, flesh can become holy.

That changes how we see everything. Human touch, human speech, human compassion—all can now carry divine power. When Christ heals the blind by touching their eyes or raises the dead with a word, He is not performing magic. He is revealing that the physical world is no longer separate from the spiritual. His very body is the place of encounter—the true temple where divinity and humanity meet.

John's Gospel captures this with unparalleled clarity. It begins not with Bethlehem but with eternity: "In the beginning was the Word, and the Word was with God, and the Word was God." The same Word that spoke light into darkness now steps into that darkness Himself. Creation was made through Him; redemption will be made by Him entering His creation. The One who once said, "Let there be light," now says, "I am the Light of the world."

In this, the Incarnation reveals the sheer coherence of God's plan. Everything He does in creation anticipates what He will do in redemption. The God who formed Adam from dust now forms Himself from the same dust through Mary. The God who breathed life into man now breathes that life again into fallen humanity. The story comes full circle.

But if the Incarnation fulfills creation, it also exposes our misunderstanding of power. We imagine that if God became man, He would come in splendour, forcing the world to its knees. Instead, He comes as a baby. The omnipotent becomes powerless, not to demonstrate weakness but to redefine strength. True power, the kind that moves heaven and earth, is love willing to suffer.

THE INCARNATION: WHEN GOD STEPPED IN

This inversion of expectations runs through Christ's entire life. His birth is in poverty, His companions are fishermen, His throne is a cross. Everything about Him confounds human categories. The God of glory hides Himself in ordinariness so that no one might be afraid to approach. The Word who could command galaxies instead whispers forgiveness to sinners.

That humility is not a tactic; it is truth. The Incarnation reveals that humility is the language of divinity. Pride builds towers toward heaven; humility brings heaven down to earth. The Creator stoops lower than any creature so that none may fall beneath His reach.

And yet, in His stooping, He never ceases to be majestic. The Gospels show this duality constantly: the carpenter's son calming storms, the weary traveller feeding multitudes, the condemned man forgiving executioners. Power and poverty coexist in perfect harmony. The infinite operates through the finite. The human body becomes the instrument of divine action.

This is why Jesus can say to the paralytic, "Your sins are forgiven," and the crowd is outraged. Only God can forgive sins. But God is standing before them in human form. The Incarnation makes that possible. The lips that pronounce pardon are human; the authority behind them is eternal. In that single moment, heaven and earth converge in a sentence.

The same happens in every miracle. When Christ touches the sick, the divine will moves through human fingers. When He raises the dead, eternity breathes through human lungs. His humanity is not a barrier to His divinity but its channel. What He does as man, God does through Him.

The Incarnation, therefore, is the key to understanding every act of Jesus. He is not a prophet acting for God but God acting through humanity. When He prays, He prays as man; when He answers prayer, He acts as God. When He suffers, He suffers as man; when He redeems,

He redeems as God. The two natures are never mixed, yet never apart.

And this is the wonder: by uniting Himself to humanity, Christ dignifies not only the flesh He took, but the flesh we bear. The human story is no longer a tragedy but a calling. If God has walked our soil, then our soil is holy. If He has wept our tears, then our tears can become sacred. If He has died our death, then our death can become doorway, not disaster.

This is what theologians mean when they say that the Incarnation "recapitulates" humanity. In Christ, God retells the story of the human race—but this time, without sin. Where Adam fell through disobedience, Christ stands through obedience. Where Eve reached for the forbidden fruit, Mary opens her hands in surrender. The garden is revisited, the test reversed. Humanity's long rebellion begins to unwind in a single act of divine humility.

Athanasius described this beautifully: "The Word of God came in His own person, because it was He alone, the image of the Father, who could recreate man made after that image." God, having made us in His likeness, now restores that likeness by taking it Himself.

The Incarnation, then, is both healing and new creation. It is not only forgiveness for what was broken but transformation into something higher. The human and divine are not merely reconciled—they are united, and through that union, humanity is elevated beyond its original state. We are not just restored to Eden; we are invited into heaven.

All this begins not with a sermon or a thunderclap but with a mother's consent and a child's cry. The greatest miracle in history begins quietly, because love rarely announces itself with spectacle.

From the first moment of His conception, the new Adam begins to reverse the tragedy of the first. Where the old humanity began with grasping, the new begins with surrender. "Behold the handmaid of the Lord," Mary says, and her fiat opens a door no sin could close.

Through her obedience, God enters His creation not by storm but by invitation. Heaven waits for human consent, and when it comes, the Word becomes flesh.

That single moment explains everything that follows. The Incarnation is not just God rescuing man from ruin—it is God inviting man to cooperate in redemption. Grace does not crush freedom; it restores it. The salvation of the world begins with a yes, and that yes echoes through every soul that receives Him.

When the eternal Son takes on flesh, He does not appear in isolation but in relationship: born into a family, under the Law, within a culture. In this, the Incarnation reveals how deeply God respects the order He created. He does not bypass human history; He enters it. He sanctifies it from within. The Son who spoke to Moses on Sinai now learns the Torah from Joseph's lips. The one who authored humanity's story now lives it line by line.

That descent into ordinary life is deliberate. God comes not as a conqueror to overwhelm but as a child to invite. He does not command worship; He awakens love. By living a fully human life, He touches every dimension of ours. His hands learn calluses; His back bears strain; His heart knows friendship, loneliness, laughter, and grief. Nothing human is alien to Him.

In this, the Incarnation reveals not only God's humility but His empathy. The Creator doesn't save us from suffering by avoiding it—He saves us through suffering by sharing it. The one who made the nerves of the body feels them break. The one who gave us tears allows them to fall from His own eyes. "We do not have a high priest who is unable to sympathize with our weaknesses," writes the author of Hebrews, "but one who has been tempted in every way as we are, yet without sin."

That "without sin" matters. For Christ's identification with us is complete but not compromising. He enters our condition without sharing our corruption. He lives within the constraints of time, hunger, pain, and fatigue, yet His will remains perfectly aligned with the Father's. He experiences temptation, but never consent to evil. His humanity is what ours was meant to be—integrated, luminous, obedient.

The purpose of this perfect obedience is not to shame us but to heal us. In every act of Christ's human life, divine grace restores what sin destroyed. His obedience undoes Adam's rebellion; His purity untangles human lust; His compassion reverses our indifference; His trust in the Father heals our suspicion. Every virtue He lives restores a corner of the fallen human heart.

And yet, the Incarnation is not merely about moral example. Jesus doesn't come primarily to show us how to live but to give us the power to live that way. His example would only condemn us if His grace did not accompany it. But because He shares our nature, His obedience becomes ours by participation. When we are united to Him by faith and baptism, His life flows through ours as the sap through the vine. The Incarnation makes sanctification possible because it makes communion possible.

This is why the sacraments matter so deeply. They are not magic rituals or empty symbols; they are the continuation of the Incarnation through time. Just as the divine entered the human in the womb of Mary, so divinity continues to enter matter in baptismal water, Eucharistic bread, anointing oil. The same Word who took flesh continues to take tangible form, feeding His people with His very life.

Every encounter with grace, then, is an encounter with the Incarnate One. The Church does not merely teach about Christ; she carries Him. Her sacraments are not human inventions but extensions of His touch. "This is My body… this is My blood" is the language of the Incarnation perpetuated. The God who once dwelt in a single body now dwells in a mystical body—the Church—and through her, His life flows into the world.

That ongoing presence reveals the full scope of the Incarnation. It was never meant to be confined to thirty years in Galilee. The Word made flesh did not ascend to abandon but to extend. His human body becomes the seed of a new humanity. The Church, animated by His Spirit, is the continuation of His incarnate mission. In her, the divine continues to meet the human, just as surely as it did in Him.

This is why Christianity is not simply belief in a doctrine but participation in a person. To be saved is not to be convinced by arguments but to be united to Christ. The Incarnation is the door to that union. It is the means by which the infinite becomes accessible, the invisible becomes tangible, and the transcendent becomes near.

And yet, many struggle with this idea because it seems too human. They want a God who remains pure spirit, untouched by our mess. But a God who will not touch the dirt cannot heal it. A distant deity may inspire awe, but only an incarnate God can inspire love. It is one thing to admire omnipotence from afar; it is another to embrace mercy that kneels beside you in the mud.

The Incarnation tells us that God's plan is not escape from humanity but its redemption. The flesh that once led us astray becomes the instrument of salvation. The body that sinned becomes the temple of the Spirit. The same nature that fell in Adam is raised in Christ. The Word doesn't erase what He made; He refashions it.

That is why the Church has always resisted the idea that salvation means fleeing the material world. Christianity is not Gnosticism. It doesn't promise escape into pure spirit but resurrection of the body. The goal is not to leave earth behind but to renew it. "Behold," says Christ in Revelation, "I make all things new."

The Incarnation is the down payment on that renewal. The same body that was born in Bethlehem, crucified at Calvary, and raised in glory is the pattern for the destiny of all who belong to Him. As Paul writes, "He will transform our lowly bodies to be like His glorious body." The flesh that God assumed is the flesh He glorified. In that promise, every scar of suffering, every tear of grief, every weary act of love finds its meaning.

So when we ask why God became man, the answer is both cosmic and personal. He became man to save the world, yes—but also to save *you*. To enter your weakness, to lift your failures into His strength, to make your humanity radiant with His divinity. The Incarnation is not a theory about God; it is God's hand reaching for yours.

When we say "God became man," we are not speaking in metaphor. We mean it literally. The eternal Word who spoke creation into existence truly entered time. He took on DNA, hunger, laughter, exhaustion. He felt the cold of night and the warmth of friendship. The mystery of the Incarnation is not a poetic way of saying God is "close to us." It is the reality that God has *joined Himself* to us in flesh and blood.

This union is not partial—it is complete. In Christ, divinity and humanity meet not like two liquids that mix and lose distinction, but like soul and body joined in one person. The divine nature is uncreated, infinite, and eternal. The human nature is created, finite, and temporal. Yet in Jesus they coexist perfectly, united without confusion or division. He is not a divine person wearing a human mask, nor a human adopted by God. He is one divine person with two complete natures.

That truth matters, because it means every action of Jesus has infinite value. When He eats, works, or prays, He is not merely performing human acts; He is infusing them with divine worth. The smallest gesture of His humanity reveals the heart of God. Every miracle, every mercy, every tear is a window into the divine. The Son of Mary and the Son of God are not two beings sharing space—they are one and the same person.

This is the logic of salvation: what is united to God is healed by God. When the divine life touches humanity in Christ, that contact becomes the instrument of redemption. Every fiber of His being, every thought and emotion, every movement of His will becomes a channel of grace. As the Fathers often said, "He healed what He assumed." By assuming our nature completely, He heals it completely—from within.

Think of how the Incarnation answers our deepest fears about God. For centuries humanity imagined the divine as distant, untouchable, maybe benevolent but ultimately beyond sympathy. In Christ, God is no longer an abstraction. He has a face, a voice, and a history. He is not the god of philosophers but the God who walks dusty roads, who kneels to wash feet, who stretches out His arms to embrace the world.

This is why the Gospels are not philosophical treatises but personal encounters. The woman at the well, the leper, the centurion, the thief—all meet God in flesh. Theology becomes biography. The infinite love that once seemed unreachable now looks into human eyes and calls by name.

But the Incarnation is not only revelation; it is reconciliation. The birth of Christ is already the beginning of His passion. From the moment He enters the world, He begins to bear its weight. His cry in the manger is the first echo of His cry on the Cross. The shadow of Calvary stretches all the way to Bethlehem.

Why? Because the same flesh that nurses at Mary's breast is the flesh that will be pierced for the world's salvation. The Incarnation is the precondition for the Crucifixion. God could not die; man could. So God became man precisely so that He might die—not as a tragic victim but as a willing Redeemer.

Anselm's principle—"only man should pay, only God could pay"—finds its fulfilment here. Humanity owes a debt of love it cannot repay; divinity has the means but not the obligation. In Christ, both come together: the One who owes nothing pays everything.

The cross is not divine overreaction but divine completion. It is love carried to its logical conclusion.

And this is the beauty of the Incarnation: God's justice and mercy are not competing forces but one act of love. The very nature that sinned is the nature that now offers reparation. The very body that suffered the curse now becomes the channel of blessing. The same humanity that turned from God now becomes the bridge back to Him.

This is why Christ calls Himself the "way." He is not merely a teacher of the way; He *is* the way. His person—the union of divine and human—is the living road across the abyss of sin. Every step He takes on earth is a step toward closing that distance. Every word He speaks is divine truth in human tones, every miracle a flash of heaven breaking through.

And when we say that Christ's death has infinite value, it is because of this union. The one who suffers on the Cross is not a man separated from God but God in human flesh. The nails pierce mortal hands, but those hands belong to the eternal Word. The blood that flows down the wood is human blood, yet it is also the blood of the Creator. That is why it can redeem not just one life, but all.

Here we glimpse the sheer precision of divine love. God saves not by cancelling justice but by fulfilling it from within. He does not destroy the human story; He rewrites it from the inside. The Word who once said, "Let there be light," now says, "It is finished," and both are acts of creation. The same voice that spoke the world into being now speaks it into redemption.

The Incarnation also explains the intimacy of salvation. Because Christ shares our humanity, He is not just an external saviour who rescues from afar. He is the vine into which we are grafted, the head whose life flows into every member of His body. Redemption is not a legal exchange but a living connection. We are saved not by transaction but by transformation—by participation in His life.

When you pray, when you receive the sacraments, when you love, you are not merely imitating Jesus; you are sharing in His own divine-human life. His humanity becomes the medium of grace—the conduit by which His divinity reaches ours. This is why the Church calls the Eucharist "the medicine of immortality." The same Word who took flesh now gives that flesh as food. The Incarnation did not end in Bethlehem; it continues at every altar.

Without this understanding, Christianity becomes either moralism or myth. If Jesus were only a good man, His death would be martyrdom, not salvation. If He were only God appearing as man, His life would be theatre, not redemption. But because He is both, His every word and wound become eternity touching time.

The mystery is as vast as it is practical. When you kneel to pray, the God who hears you knows what human knees feel like. When you suffer loss, the God who comforts you has stood at gravesides. When you are betrayed, the God who redeems you has felt the kiss of a traitor. There is no cry you can utter that He cannot understand from within.

That is why the Incarnation is not simply doctrine—it is comfort. It means that no suffering is wasted, no humanity is forgotten, no heart is beyond reach. The infinite has entered the finite, and nothing finite will ever be the same again.

If the Incarnation were only about revelation—showing us what God is like—it would already be extraordinary. But it goes further. It doesn't just show who God is; it shows what humanity is meant to be. The Word didn't become flesh merely to visit creation but to raise it. In Him, we see not only divinity revealed but humanity restored.

From the very first breath in Bethlehem to the final cry on Calvary, Jesus lives the human life as it was designed to be lived—in perfect communion with the Father. He does nothing independently, not because He lacks freedom, but because His freedom is perfect obedience. "My food is to do the will of Him who sent Me," He says. In Christ, human will and divine will are united without friction. That is the true image of man: not self-assertion but self-giving.

The Incarnation thus redefines greatness. Power is no longer measured by how high one rises but by how low one stoops in love. When the eternal Word kneels to wash the feet of His disciples, the world glimpses the deepest truth about God and man alike: the one who serves is the one who reigns. The Creator's majesty shines most brightly in humility.

This is not sentimental moralism. It is metaphysical reality. The humility of Christ is the revelation of divine being itself. God is love—and love, by its nature, gives itself away. The Incarnation is not a departure from God's nature but its perfect expression. The Father gives the Son; the Son gives Himself to the world; the Spirit gives life. Creation, redemption, and sanctification are all extensions of that same movement of self-giving love.

That is why the Incarnation is not simply a single historical event but the centre of all history. Every moment before it moves toward it; every moment after flows from it. It is the still point where eternity touches time. In Christ, past and future converge, heaven and earth are reconciled, God and man are made one.

It's no accident that the birth of Christ splits history in two—before and after. The timeline of the world bends around a manger. The Incarnation is the fulcrum on which all creation balances. Without it, the universe remains divided; with it, everything begins to cohere.

This unity is not abstract. It is personal. In Christ, every fragment of existence is gathered and reconnected to its source. The atoms of His body belong to this world, yet the life animating them belongs to eternity. He is the bridge in flesh, the meeting place of heaven and earth.

This is why the early Fathers called Him the *Mediator* not just of salvation but of creation itself. The same Word through whom all things were made now enters what He made to restore it from within.

Redemption is creation renewed; salvation is Genesis repeated in glory. "Behold, I make all things new," He declares, and He means it literally.

Through the Incarnation, time itself changes character. Before Christ, time was a march toward death. After Christ, it becomes the arena of grace. Every moment now has potential for communion with the eternal. God has not only entered human history; He has filled it with Himself. The mundane can become miraculous, the ordinary sacramental. A mother's love, a worker's labour, a sufferer's pain—all can participate in divine life because God has lived them.

This is why Christianity alone can say, with both realism and hope, that creation is good yet broken, fallen yet redeemable. The same God who made the world has stepped into it, not to destroy but to heal. No philosophy or religion ever dared claim so much. The gods of the pagans demanded escape from matter; the philosophies of men sought liberation from the body. Only Christianity says that matter itself can be glorified, that the body can be resurrected, that the world can be transfigured.

That conviction flows directly from the Incarnation. Because God has taken flesh, flesh can now take God. The material world becomes the theatre of salvation. That's why Christianity builds hospitals instead of escape cults, cathedrals instead of caves. The believer does not flee creation; he consecrates it.

And yet, for all its cosmic grandeur, the Incarnation is deeply personal. The Word became flesh not just to renew humanity in general but to enter each individual's story. His descent is as intimate as it is infinite. He comes not merely to dwell *among* us but *within* us.

When the angel tells Mary, "The Holy Spirit will come upon you, and the power of the Most High will overshadow you," those words describe not only her vocation but ours. Every believer, by grace, becomes a dwelling place of God. The same Spirit that conceived Christ in her womb now conceives Christ in the soul. The Incarnation continues, invisibly but really, wherever faith welcomes Him.

This is the mystery Paul describes when he writes, "Christ in you, the hope of glory." The Incarnation is not past tense; it is present reality. It is the pattern of salvation repeated in every soul: God enters, grace grows, life is born.

That is also why Christianity is not primarily a system of morals but a life of communion. The goal is not to imitate Jesus from afar but to live His life from within. The Incarnation makes that possible. Because God became what we are, we can become what He is—not in essence but in participation. The divine life, once inaccessible, now flows through our humanity.

This union transforms not only individuals but the entire human family. The Son of God has united Himself with every human nature, and therefore every human being is touched by His redemptive act. No life is untouched by the Incarnation, even if unaware of it. The grace unleashed by His descent fills all time and space.

This is what Paul means when he writes, "As in Adam all die, so in Christ shall all be made alive." Adam's disobedience fractured humanity; Christ's obedience restores it. In Him, the human race begins again. He is the new Adam, the head of a new creation.

And this new creation is not distant; it begins here and now. Every act of love participates in it. Every work of mercy manifests it. Every soul transformed by grace extends the reach of the Incarnation. God's presence is no longer confined to one body in one place. Through His Spirit, the Incarnate Word lives in millions of hearts, continuing His mission through them.

This is what it means when the Church says she is "the Body of Christ." It is not metaphor. The same divine life that animated the man Jesus animates His people. The Incarnation has multiplied through history, turning believers into living extensions of the Word made flesh.

THE INCARNATION: WHEN GOD STEPPED IN

That is the astonishing consequence of the mystery we celebrate at Christmas: God has become man so that man, united to Him, might carry God into the world.

The Incarnation, then, is not simply the centre of Christian doctrine — it is the centre of reality itself. Everything in heaven and on earth, seen and unseen, orbits this one event: God made flesh. The galaxies exist by the Word who once lay in a manger; the laws of physics hold because the same Word holds them in being. The mystery of Christ is not one story among others; it is the story behind all stories.

If we look back now at all that came before — creation, the Fall, the Law, the prophets — we can see what they were pointing toward. God had been descending step by step into His world: from the voice in Eden to the fire on Sinai, from the glory in the temple to the whisper in the prophets. Every step was a preparation for the moment when He would no longer come as presence but as person. The Incarnation is the final descent, the point where the Creator enters creation completely.

And yet, in that descent, He does not diminish His glory; He displays it. "We have seen His glory," John writes, "the glory as of the only Son from the Father, full of grace and truth." The glory of God is no longer blinding light but humble love. The majesty of heaven now shines in mercy, in the patient strength of one who bears the weight of the world on His shoulders.

This is the revelation that changes everything: that divine glory and human weakness are not opposites but allies. In Christ, omnipotence expresses itself as vulnerability. The hands that shaped the stars are the same hands that wash feet. The One who commands angels allows Himself to be held by sinners. Love has revealed its final secret — that it is strongest when it stoops.

For this reason, the Incarnation remains the permanent answer to every human question. To the philosopher asking what is truth, God answers: *Truth is a person*. To the sufferer asking where God is, He answers: *I am here, in your pain.* To the sinner asking if forgiveness is possible, He answers: *I have already carried your sin in My body.* To the seeker wondering how to reach heaven, He answers: *Heaven has already come to you.*

The Incarnation reveals not only who God is, but what salvation is. Salvation is not escape from the world; it is the world remade. It is not absorption into divinity, but communion with it. It is not the abandonment of the human, but its transfiguration. The Word became flesh not to erase humanity but to perfect it.

This is why Jesus remains forever both God and man. In Him, heaven and earth are no longer separate categories; they are one reality united in love. His humanity is the door through which divinity enters the world, and our humanity becomes the door through which we enter God. Every grace flows through that bridge, every prayer passes along it, every soul that reaches heaven walks across it.

That is the meaning of Christ's words, "I am the way, and the truth, and the life." He is not one way among others; He is the only bridge between creature and Creator, because He alone spans both sides. Without the Incarnation, there is no way, no truth, no life — only longing.

And yet, because of it, the world is filled with possibility. Every kindness, every act of faith, every cry for mercy now resonates with eternal significance. The Incarnation means that history is not a meaningless cycle but a story moving toward redemption. The same God who entered time will one day enter it again to complete what He began.

For now, He continues to dwell with us sacramentally. The Christ who once walked the roads of Galilee now walks the world through His Church. Her hands anoint, her words forgive, her table feeds, because the Word made flesh still speaks, still heals, still gives Himself. The Incarnation did not end when the body of Christ ascended; it expanded.

The humanity He took from Mary is now distributed, mystically, across His people.

Every Mass is a continuation of Bethlehem: God hidden in matter, offering Himself as food. Every confession is a continuation of Nazareth: God dwelling quietly in human hearts. Every act of mercy is a continuation of Calvary: God pouring Himself out in love. The mystery never ended — it only multiplied.

And this mystery is the key to everything that follows. Without the Incarnation, the Cross would be cruelty and the Resurrection a dream. With it, they become the logic of love carried to its conclusion. The same body that was born of Mary will hang on the tree; the same flesh that lay in a manger will rise from the tomb. Salvation is not the cancellation of flesh but its glorification.

The Incarnation assures us that nothing human is beyond redemption. Every scar can become a wound of glory. Every failure can be transfigured by grace. Every death, in Him, can become doorway to life.

That is why the Church insists — not arrogantly, but joyfully — that Christ is the only way to God. There can be no other, because no other is both God and man. No prophet, no sage, no saint could bridge that gap. Only the one who made the chasm could cross it. Only the one who holds infinity in one hand and mortality in the other could join them.

This exclusivity is not exclusion; it is invitation. Because there is one Mediator, there is hope for all. Because the bridge is singular, it spans everything. The Incarnation is not narrow; it is universal in scope. The arms of the God-Man stretch wide enough to embrace the whole world.

When you understand this, the faith ceases to be a rulebook and becomes a revelation. Christianity is not a philosophy of morals or a system of rituals; it is the encounter with a person — the God who has stepped into history, taken on our flesh, and never left.

That is the claim that no other religion dares to make: that the Infinite became one of us, not in myth or symbol, but in fact. The Word became flesh — and stayed flesh. He did not visit; He abides.

And so the story of the Incarnation ends as it began — with wonder. A virgin conceives. A carpenter raises the Son of God. Shepherds hear angels. The Creator lies in a feeding trough, and heaven sings. This is the moment when eternity breathes in time.

It is also the moment that reveals who we are. We are creatures capable of God, made for communion, redeemed for glory. The Incarnation is not just God's coming to man; it is God's declaration of what man was made to be — the dwelling place of divine love.

From this point on, everything will change. The light has entered the darkness, and the darkness cannot overcome it. The God who walked among us will soon walk the road to the Cross. The Word that took flesh will let that flesh be broken, so that all flesh may be healed.

The Incarnation was the beginning of salvation. The next chapter will show its fulfillment. The child who was born to die will reveal, on Calvary, the cost and the victory of divine love.

For now, it is enough to know this: the Infinite has stepped inside the finite — and stayed.

4

The Cross: The Price of Love

The Cross stands at the centre of the Christian faith — not as ornament or metaphor, but as the axis on which the universe turns. If the Incarnation is God stepping into the story, the Cross is the chapter where He pays the cost of love written in blood. There is no Christianity without it, because there is no salvation without it. Remove the Cross, and everything collapses into sentimentality: love without justice, mercy without meaning, forgiveness without truth.

People often ask, "Why the Cross? Why suffering? Why blood?" Why couldn't God, if He is truly loving, simply forgive? The question feels compassionate, but beneath it lies a misunderstanding — that forgiveness is mere leniency. Yet mercy without truth is not mercy; it's indifference. A world in which evil goes unaccounted for would not be healed, only hidden. The Cross exists because God takes both love and justice seriously. He will not call evil good, but neither will He allow evil to have the last word.

From the beginning, humanity has sensed that sin requires sacrifice. Ancient altars across cultures testify to this intuition. When we do wrong, something breaks — in us, between us, and before God. Blood is the symbol of life, and so blood became the language of reparation.

The pagan guessed dimly what revelation makes clear: the cost of sin is life itself. The difference is that in Christianity, the altar is reversed. It is no longer man offering sacrifice to reach God; it is God offering Himself to reach man.

Sin is not a clerical error that can be erased from a ledger. It is a rupture in being, a cosmic treason against the Source of life. To "let it go" would be to make God unjust, to deny His own holiness. Yet to destroy sinners outright would be to contradict His love. The dilemma seems impossible until we see what God does at Calvary: He bears in Himself what justice demands so that mercy can triumph without deceit.

Saint Paul says it with devastating simplicity: "He Himself bore our sins in His body on the tree." The Judge becomes the victim. The offended takes the place of the offender. Justice and mercy, instead of cancelling each other, kiss in the pierced heart of Christ.

But we must be careful here. The Cross is not divine child abuse, as some critics suggest, nor a Father venting wrath upon an innocent Son. The Father and the Son are not adversaries but one in will and love. The Father's justice and the Son's obedience are not two competing impulses but one movement of divine compassion. "God was in Christ reconciling the world to Himself," Paul writes — not punishing a third party, but absorbing the punishment Himself. The Cross is God's self-offering to satisfy His own justice.

This is why the Crucifixion is not an accident of politics or the failure of a prophet. It is the culmination of the Incarnation. God took flesh precisely so that He could offer it. The manger and the Cross are made of the same wood. The baby who cried in Bethlehem came to cry again on Golgotha — not because He was overpowered, but because He chose to love to the end.

In every generation, the Cross offends both moral pride and human sentiment. To the proud, it seems unnecessary — surely we can redeem ourselves through effort and virtue. To the sentimental, it seems cruel — surely love should not bleed. Yet the Cross answers both illusions. To the first, it declares that sin is too deep for self-cure. To the second, it declares that love is too real to stay comfortable.

If we could save ourselves, Christ's suffering would be absurd. But if sin is what Scripture says it is — the death of the soul, the fracture of creation — then only divine intervention could repair it. The Cross is not Plan B; it is the only plan that could work. "Without the shedding of blood," says Hebrews, "there is no forgiveness of sins." That is not a demand of a vengeful deity but the logic of a moral universe: life must answer for death, love must bear the cost of hate.

The ancient Church understood this as the mystery of substitution and participation. Christ stands in our place, not as an external substitute who shields us from punishment, but as the new Adam in whom we all are represented. When He dies, the human race dies with Him; when He rises, humanity rises renewed. "He became what we are," wrote Irenaeus, "so that we might become what He is." Redemption is not an exchange of paperwork; it is a re-creation of humanity from within.

This is why the Cross cannot be reduced to a legal transaction. It is not a cold settlement of accounts but a burning act of love. The Son does not endure suffering to change the Father's heart; He endures it to change ours. The Cross reveals not the cruelty of God but the seriousness of sin and the extent of mercy. At Calvary, we see both what we have done to God and what God has done for us.

Look at the scene. The Creator of the world hangs between heaven and earth — rejected by the world He made, abandoned by the friends He loved. Nails pierce the hands that healed, thorns crown the head that blessed, and yet from His lips comes not condemnation but prayer: "Father, forgive them." No philosopher ever conceived such logic; no religion dared imagine such a God. Here is love that absorbs hatred, justice that satisfies itself through compassion.

The Cross, then, is not merely the price of forgiveness; it is the revelation of love's nature. Love, if it is real, must be willing to bear pain for the beloved. In every act of true love, something dies — pride, comfort, self-interest. The Cross is that principle taken to infinity. God's love becomes tangible because it becomes vulnerable.

That is what makes the Cross unavoidable. We can debate theology, ethics, miracles, but the Cross stops every argument. It is God's final word to the world — the word not of explanation but of demonstration. "God proves His love for us," Paul says, "in that while we were still sinners, Christ died for us."

Beneath that beam, excuses die. Our pretence that we are "good enough" shatters in the face of this necessity. If forgiveness required such a price, sin must be more than weakness; it must be death. But beneath that same beam, despair also dies. If God loved us enough to pay that price Himself, then no sinner is too far gone.

This is the tension every soul must face when it looks at the Crucified: this is what my sin costs — and this is how much I am worth. The Cross is the mirror that shows both our guilt and our glory. It humbles us to dust and lifts us to heaven in the same breath.

Stand long enough beneath the Cross, and something profound happens: the event ceases to be distant history and becomes revelation. The longer we gaze, the clearer it becomes that this is not an accident of cruelty but the deliberate act of divine logic. Every beam of that wood, every drop of blood, speaks of necessity—not the necessity of fate, but of love's integrity.

Love must take sin seriously. Mercy must satisfy justice. God's holiness cannot be compromised, because it is the very condition of love's truth. To "just forgive" without cost would make evil irrelevant. It would declare that betrayal and fidelity, cruelty and compassion, matter equally. A God who could overlook injustice would be no better than the tyrants He condemns.

That is why the Cross stands where it does—at the intersection of justice and mercy. Divine love refuses to ignore what we have done, but it also refuses to leave us to its consequences. At Calvary, God does not choose between punishment and pardon; He unites them. Justice is fulfilled, not by condemnation, but by substitution. The innocent suffers for the guilty—not to appease wrath, but to extinguish it.

Saint Paul expresses this paradox with surgical clarity: "For our sake, He made Him to be sin who knew no sin, so that in Him we might become the righteousness of God." (2 Corinthians 5:21). Notice the symmetry—sin and righteousness, substitution and participation. Christ does not merely take our place; He takes us into Himself. He doesn't erase our debt from outside the system; He enters the broken system and transforms it from within.

Theologians have wrestled for centuries to express this mystery. Anselm called it "satisfaction"—the idea that only God could repay the infinite debt owed to God, yet only humanity *should* repay it. Therefore, the one who is both must make satisfaction on behalf of both. Others, like Irenaeus and Athanasius, preferred the language of *recapitulation*: Christ becomes the new Adam, reliving the human story in perfect obedience, redeeming every moment the first Adam ruined. These theories do not contradict but complement each other, showing that the Cross is both courtroom and creation, both reparation and renewal.

Yet to many, this still feels abstract. We want to know why blood, why pain, why the spectacle of suffering. Couldn't God have forgiven with a word? He could have, if forgiveness were a mere decree. But sin is not a legal problem; it's a relational one. It's not a rule broken but a bond broken, a trust violated, a love betrayed. The wound is not on parchment but in persons. Words alone cannot heal that. Only a person can.

The Cross, then, is the visible form of invisible love. God becomes man so that love can bleed, so that mercy can take a body and meet evil face to face. When nails pierce His hands, it is not divine wrath that drives them, but divine love that permits them. He bears what justice demands, not out of compulsion but compassion.

This is the heart of the mystery: the Son's obedience is not servitude; it is self-giving. He is not crushed by the Father's anger but propelled by the Father's love. The Cross is the eternal will of God translated into time—"God so loved the world that He gave His only Son." The giving is not loss but revelation.

Think of it this way: the Cross is not what love *suffers*; it is what love *does*. It is love's own shape when faced with sin. Because love always seeks the beloved, it will chase even into death. Jesus descends to where man has fallen, not simply to sympathize but to lift him out. "No one takes My life from Me," He says, "I lay it down of My own accord." The Crucifixion is not murder of the innocent but the self-offering of the Holy.

The language of Scripture reinforces this. Jesus is both priest and victim, offering Himself "once for all" (Hebrews 9:26). The altar is not a place of divine cruelty but of divine exchange—our death given to Him, His life given to us. The Lamb of God does not appease a wrathful deity; He reveals a God whose wrath against sin is nothing other than His passion for justice, His refusal to leave the world enslaved.

Justice, in the biblical sense, is not retribution but restoration—the right ordering of relationship. At the Cross, that order is restored. Humanity, once alienated, is reconciled; creation, once fractured, begins to heal. The punishment of sin—death—is absorbed by the only one who can survive it. He drinks the cup to its dregs so that none of us need taste it unredeemed.

But the Cross is not merely transaction; it is transformation. God doesn't only remove guilt; He makes us new. The blood that cleanses also consecrates. In baptism, we are "buried with Him into death," and in the Eucharist, we drink the life that conquered death. Salvation is not just something done *for* us; it is something done *in* us. The Cross is not a receipt for pardon; it is a seed planted in the human soul, growing into resurrection.

The beauty of this truth is that it reframes the meaning of suffering itself. Because the Son of God suffered, suffering is no longer meaningless. Because He carried the Cross, our own crosses can now carry grace. Every sorrow offered in love becomes participation in His redemption. This is why Christ says, "Take up your cross and follow Me." He is not glorifying pain; He is revealing purpose. Pain that is united to love is not wasted—it becomes the raw material of salvation.

At the same time, the Cross is the judgment of the world. Jesus Himself says, "Now is the judgment of this world; now will the ruler of this world be cast out." At Calvary, sin, death, and Satan are exposed for what they are—parasites feeding on goodness. The Cross unmasks evil's impotence. The enemy can destroy flesh but not love; he can take life but not meaning. The very weapon meant for defeat becomes the instrument of victory.

This is why the Cross, for the early Christians, was never simply a symbol of suffering but of triumph. They saw it as the Tree of Life replanted in the centre of the world. Where Adam's disobedience brought death through a tree, Christ's obedience brings life through another. The fruit of that tree is the Eucharist, the body broken yet glorified, the same love made edible.

To those outside the faith, this sounds foolish — and Paul admitted as much. "The message of the Cross is foolishness to those who are perishing, but to us who are being saved it is the power of God." The world measures wisdom by success, but the Cross redefines success as sacrifice. The world measures power by control, but the Cross reveals power as self-giving love.

And this is precisely why we cannot soften it. The Cross is meant to shock. It offends the intellect that demands comfort and the ego that demands independence. It declares that salvation is not self-improvement but surrender, not human ascent but divine descent. It tells us that God takes our sin more seriously than we do and loves us more fiercely than we dare believe.

The Cross is not God's reaction to sin; it is His response. Reaction is compulsion; response is freedom. The Cross is the free act of the God who loves to the end.

The Cross confronts every assumption the human heart makes about God and about itself. It tells us that evil is not a minor flaw in the system but a fatal disease; that goodness cannot be manufactured; and that love, to be real, must be costly. Every worldview that denies these truths eventually drifts into denial or despair. The Cross alone keeps both justice and hope alive in the same universe.

If the Incarnation was the moment God stepped into history, the Cross is the moment history turned inside out. What looked like defeat was victory in disguise. What appeared as humiliation was exaltation. "When I am lifted up," Jesus said, "I will draw all people to Myself." The lifting up He spoke of was not a throne but a gibbet. Yet that instrument of death became the magnet of salvation. The Cross is the point where the world's cruelty becomes God's compassion.

No wonder the earliest Christians spoke of it in paradoxes. Paul called it a "stumbling block to Jews and folly to Gentiles." Peter called it "precious." John called it "glory." For them, the Cross was not a tragedy to be mourned but a mystery to be adored. They saw in the crucified Christ not the ruin of divine power but its revelation. Omnipotence chose weakness to defeat strength, and truth used silence to confound lies.

To understand that, we have to abandon the logic of power. The world admires control, success, and dominance. God reveals Himself through surrender, failure, and obedience. The world exalts winners;

heaven crowns martyrs. The Cross overturns every hierarchy of pride. It teaches that the only victory worth having is the one that gives itself away.

That's why the Cross is not simply an event to believe in but a pattern to live by. "If anyone would come after Me," Jesus says, "let him deny himself, take up his cross, and follow Me." That command is not masochism; it's realism. To love in a fallen world is to suffer. To forgive is to bleed. Every act of mercy costs something. When we bear wrong patiently, forgive an enemy, or choose truth over comfort, we participate in the same logic that saved the world.

This is what theologians call "redemptive participation." Christ redeems *by* suffering; we are redeemed *into* His suffering. His passion becomes the grammar of our own lives. In baptism, we are united with His death; in Eucharist, we share His life; in every trial accepted in faith, His Cross touches ours. This is not poetic language but ontological reality. The life of grace is cruciform because divine love is cruciform.

It is also why Christian joy has a strange shape. It isn't naïve optimism or stoic endurance. It is the serenity that knows love wins even when it bleeds. The saints smile from the scaffold and sing in prison not because they enjoy pain but because they see what pain can become. The Cross transforms suffering from meaningless chaos into seed of glory. Every Good Friday hides an Easter Sunday.

Still, the mystery of the Cross remains: why *this* way? Could God not have chosen a gentler path? The question only arises if we forget what was at stake. The problem wasn't ignorance; it was enmity. Humanity had declared war on God. The very nature of our rebellion meant that reconciliation could not come by advice or persuasion. It required an act of self-giving that reversed the direction of the universe. God had to enter the space of alienation and redeem it from the inside.

That's what happens on Calvary. The Son of God steps into the darkest possible distance from the Father — not in essence, but in experience. "My God, My God, why have You forsaken Me?" He cries, quoting the psalm that begins in despair and ends in praise. He does not lose the Father; He plumbs the depth of human estrangement so that no sinner ever need say those words alone.

The Cross, then, is solidarity taken to its limit. It is divine empathy perfected — not pity from afar, but presence within the wound. God suffers *with* us so that He can heal *in* us. He does not offer comfort by bypassing pain but by entering it and transforming it. The Almighty becomes the condemned, the Holy becomes sin, the Healer becomes the wounded — so that in every human wound, His healing might begin.

No other religion even approaches this claim. In every myth and philosophy, the gods remain untouchable. They may instruct, punish, or reward, but they never *bleed*. The Cross is Christianity's audacious uniqueness: divinity not only feeling compassion but undergoing it. "The Word became flesh," John says — but at Calvary, the Word became broken flesh. And from that brokenness flowed the world's redemption.

This is what theologians mean by "substitution." Christ dies *for us* — not because God delights in death, but because love must enter the consequence of sin to undo it. "Greater love has no one than this," Jesus says, "that a man lay down his life for his friends." The Cross is that line fulfilled to infinity: the Friend of sinners laying down His life for His enemies.

But substitution in Scripture is never mechanical. It's not the case that God punished Jesus *instead* of us, as though shifting the penalty onto a third party. It's that God in Christ took humanity into Himself and let sin expend itself against infinite love. In other words, He didn't stand between the bullet and the victim; He stepped inside the victim and absorbed the bullet from within. This is why Paul says we are "crucified with Christ." His death isn't merely representative — it's participatory. We were there, in Him, when it happened.

That truth is made visible in the sacraments. In baptism, we pass through water that symbolizes death and resurrection — our old life drowned, our new life rising with Him. In Eucharist, we eat the same body that hung on the Cross; His sacrifice becomes our sustenance. Grace is not an abstract favour; it is the life of the Crucified pulsing in our veins.

When you begin to grasp this, salvation stops feeling like a transaction and starts feeling like transfiguration. The Cross is not God's demand; it's His donation. It is what happens when divine justice and divine mercy occupy the same body. The nails hold not just flesh but attributes together. Justice nails mercy to time; mercy raises justice to eternity.

This is why Jesus can cry, "It is finished." He doesn't mean "I am finished," but "the work is accomplished." The Greek word *tetelestai* carries the sense of completion, fulfillment, even perfection. The story that began in Eden — man reaching for godhood by grasping — ends with God reaching for manhood by giving. The first tree brought death; the second brings life.

The Cross, therefore, is the hinge of creation. Everything before it leans forward in hope; everything after it leans back in gratitude. Every altar ever built, every lamb ever slain, every tear ever shed in repentance converges on this one moment. Here, the justice of heaven meets the misery of earth — and heaven wins.

From heaven's vantage, the Cross is not merely an event—it is the axis of history. Every covenant of the Old Testament, every promise of mercy, every cry of the prophets, finds its "Yes" in this single act. The blood that runs down that wood is the bloodstream of Scripture itself. In it, the promise to Abraham, the Passover of Moses, the lament of David, and the suffering servant of Isaiah all converge. What was symbol in Israel becomes substance in Christ.

Consider the Passover. In Egypt, the lamb's blood marked the doorposts to save the Israelites from death. On Calvary, the true Lamb marks the wood of the Cross with His own blood—not to protect from a single night of wrath, but from eternal death itself. When John the Baptist saw Jesus and cried, "Behold the Lamb of God who takes away the sin of the world," he was naming this fulfillment. The Cross is the true Exodus: God's people freed not from Pharaoh's slavery but from sin's.

Every religion intuits the need for sacrifice, but only here does the direction reverse. Humanity has always climbed upward, offering to the divine; now God descends, offering Himself to the human. The altar of Calvary is built not on human hands but on divine humility. That's why the tearing of the temple veil at the moment of Christ's death matters. The barrier between God and man—symbolized for centuries in that thick curtain—rips from top to bottom. Heaven initiates, not earth. Access to God is now opened from above, not achieved from below.

Saint Leo the Great described it beautifully: "The Creator was found in His creature; the Lord of the universe veiled His majesty and took the form of a servant, that by one and the same act He might restore man and reveal God." In that unveiling, the Cross becomes the world's new temple, its centre of worship and reconciliation. No more priests offering the blood of animals; the High Priest Himself offers His own. The eternal Word pronounces the last word: "It is finished."

But if the Cross ends sacrifice, it also perfects it. The old offerings expressed guilt without curing it, hope without fulfillment. Calvary achieves what they anticipated—it reconciles, because it reveals. The worship of the old covenant was shadow; the worship of the new is participation. Every Mass now re-presents that one sacrifice, not as repetition but as presence. The same body once nailed now rests upon the altar, the same blood now poured into chalices. The Cross stretches into time so that every generation can drink from its side.

That side—the pierced heart of Christ—has always been seen by the Church as the wellspring of grace. From it flow blood and water, symbolizing Eucharist and Baptism, the sacraments of new life. The soldier's spear, meant to prove death, becomes the sign of birth. Out of a wound comes the Church, as Eve came from Adam's side. The price of love is not only death; it is the willingness to remain vulnerable even in glory.

For the Cross is not erased by the Resurrection; it is glorified. The risen body still bears the wounds. They are no longer open but radiant, the scars of victory. When Thomas touches them, he touches not evidence of failure but the proof of faithfulness. In those wounds, love has engraved its permanence. Heaven will never forget what it cost to bring us home.

This permanence reveals something staggering: redemption is not an afterthought. The Cross is not God's reaction to sin but the eternal plan of love. Scripture calls Christ "the Lamb slain from the foundation of the world." Before the first star was set ablaze, God had already decided to bear our darkness. Creation itself was made through the logic of the Cross: love giving life by self-gift. That's why the universe, when rightly seen, carries cruciform traces everywhere—atoms giving energy through fusion, seeds dying to bear fruit, stars collapsing to give light. Reality itself operates on the pattern of sacrificial love.

The Cross, therefore, is not against nature but its redemption. It restores creation's true rhythm. In sin, man inverted that rhythm by grasping for life rather than receiving it. The Cross reverses that inversion. Christ, by relinquishing life, restores the flow of grace to the world. His death is not destruction but divine metabolism—the transformation of death into life.

This is why Christian art, from the earliest catacombs, depicts the Cross not as horror but as tree, fountain, and throne. Artists carved vines growing from its arms, doves nesting in its branches, rivers flowing from its base. They understood that this instrument of torture had become the source of fertility for the soul. From this tree, the fruits of the Spirit—faith, hope, and love—ripen in the human heart.

And that transformation is not theoretical. It happens in every believer who allows the Cross to enter their life. To follow Christ is not to escape suffering but to be changed by it. The Cross becomes not only the price of love but its pattern. The saints did not adore pain for its own sake; they adored the love that pain revealed. When Francis of Assisi kissed the leper, when Maximilian Kolbe offered himself in Auschwitz, when a mother forgives the murderer of her child—each repeats the grammar of Calvary. Love bears cost, and in that cost reveals God.

But such love is impossible without grace. Human will alone cannot carry it. The ability to forgive, to endure, to love enemies, to offer one's life—these are not achievements but participations. The Cross that saves also strengthens; the same power that raised Christ from the dead works in those who believe. This is why Paul can write, "I have been crucified with Christ, and it is no longer I who live, but Christ who lives in me." The believer's life becomes an extension of the Cross—divine charity continuing its mission in human hearts.

Yet we must never forget: this is not metaphor. When we speak of the Cross, we are speaking of an event that happened in real time, to a real man, on a real hill. Nails tore real flesh. Blood soaked real earth. God's plan unfolded not in symbol but in history. The infinite entered the measurable, so that every drop of that blood carries infinite value. To reduce it to allegory is to empty it of power. To believe it as fact is to find the key to every sorrow.

For this reason, the Church keeps the Cross at the centre of her worship. Every Mass, every crucifix, every sign traced on the forehead or heart is a declaration that love has a cost—and that the cost has been paid. The Christian makes that sign not as superstition but as confession: "I live under the sign of love that died for me."

And so the Cross stands, ancient yet present, the one place where every contradiction in the human heart—guilt and longing, fear and hope, death and desire—finds resolution. It is both grave and gate, defeat and triumph, judgment and mercy. At its foot, the proud bow and the broken rise.

The Cross is therefore not an anomaly but the blueprint of salvation. It is love revealed as truth, and truth revealed as sacrifice. It is the summit of all revelation because it shows what God is like when He is most Himself. We often imagine divine glory as thunder, splendour, and distance, yet on Calvary glory takes the shape of endurance, fidelity, and mercy. In Christ crucified, power and tenderness become one.

To see this clearly is to see that the Cross is not just about guilt—it is about communion. Sin is not merely moral failure; it is relational exile. The Cross restores us not by legal adjustment but by reconciliation. The human race, estranged from its Creator, is embraced again. The arms stretched wide on that hill are the eternal gesture of God's welcome. "While we were enemies," writes Paul, "we were reconciled to God by the death of His Son."

Reconciliation means more than pardon. It means sharing life again. The Father does not simply erase the record of debt; He invites us back into the household. This is why Scripture so often uses family language—adoption, inheritance, sonship. We are not merely acquitted criminals; we are prodigal children carried home. The Cross is the doorway of that home. It turns punishment into pardon, and pardon into participation.

Participation—that is the heart of salvation. We are not saved by observing the Cross from afar, admiring it as a noble example. We are saved by entering into it. "If anyone would come after Me, let him take up his cross." Christianity is not the removal of suffering but the transformation of it into love. The moment we unite our wounds to His, they cease to be mere pain and become prayer.

This is the secret of the saints' serenity. They understood that the Cross is not only Christ's—it becomes ours. When Paul says, "I fill up in my body what is lacking in the sufferings of Christ," he is not claiming Christ's sacrifice was insufficient. He means that love's work continues in time through those who belong to Him. The Church's mission is to carry the Cross into every corner of the world—to make visible the same mercy that was made visible on Golgotha.

In this sense, the Cross is not only a moment of atonement but the shape of history. Each generation must decide whether to live under its shadow or turn away. Empires, ideologies, and philosophies rise and fall according to how they stand before that wood. Those who worship power crucify again the weak; those who worship truth kneel beneath the Crucified. The Cross divides not only time but hearts.

And yet, paradoxically, it also unites. In it, every form of alienation—Jew and Gentile, slave and free, man and woman—is reconciled. The vertical beam joins heaven and earth; the horizontal joins humanity to itself. The Church is born at that intersection: divine life flowing downward, human life flowing outward. This is why Christian community is not a social club but a sacramental body. It exists to extend the embrace of the Cross.

Still, for many modern minds, the Cross remains an embarrassment. It seems primitive, violent, even unnecessary. We prefer a God of tolerance to a God of nails. But tolerance cannot save; it can only ignore. The Cross does what no philosophy can: it takes evil seriously enough to destroy it without destroying us. In that paradox lies the Gospel's scandal and its beauty.

To call it scandalous is no exaggeration. The early Church faced mockery for preaching a crucified God. "Your God died on a cross," scoffed the Romans; "ours sit on thrones." The Christians replied, "Yes, and ours rose again." They understood that power divorced from love is tyranny, and love divorced from power is sentimentality. Only the Cross unites both perfectly.

At the Cross, power does not crush; it endures. Love does not merely weep; it redeems. In Jesus, divine omnipotence becomes omnipotent mercy. He conquers not by killing His enemies but by dying for them. That inversion is the very heart of the Gospel. It is why Christians can speak of the Cross as triumph. The apparent defeat is actually the exposure of evil's impotence. When the worst thing sin can do—kill God—is turned into the very means of salvation, evil is left weapon less.

This truth resounds through all creation. Nature itself bears witness on that day: darkness covers the land, the earth quakes, rocks split open. The universe reacts because its Lord is redeeming it. Even the Roman centurion, hardened by years of execution, can only whisper, "Truly this was the Son of God." The Cross unmasks reality—it shows that beneath history's chaos, divine order is at work.

That order is love. Every act of redemption flows from it. The Father sends the Son, not as executioner but as healer. The Son offers Himself, not out of submission but out of freedom. The Spirit, proceeding from both, carries the fruits of that act into hearts across time. The Cross is the Trinitarian life made visible: love giving, receiving, and returning within history. When we look upon it, we are peering into the inner life of God.

And that means salvation is not merely about forgiveness; it is about participation in that divine life. The Cross opens the Trinity to us. We are drawn into the love that passes between Father, Son, and Spirit. Grace is not a commodity purchased at Calvary; it is the life of God poured out. Every Eucharist, every absolution, every prayer of faith is a drop from that same fountain.

This is why the Church never speaks of "earning" salvation. Grace cannot be earned because it is infinite; it can only be received. The Cross proves this: humanity contributes nothing but the nails, yet receives everything—pardon, peace, and divine adoption. We are saved not by effort but by acceptance, not by merit but by mercy.

And yet, precisely because grace is gift, it demands response. To receive love that bleeds and remain unchanged is to mock it. The Cross calls for conversion—the turning of the heart toward the One who has already turned toward us. True repentance is not self-hatred but the acceptance of being loved beyond deserving.

When a soul finally grasps that, the Cross ceases to be scandal and becomes sanctuary. The believer no longer sees only suffering, but homecoming. In that pierced side, every exile finds shelter. The Cross is the proof that the story of the world is not tragedy but redemption.

At the heart of every question about the Cross lies one deeper still: *Who is this God?*

If the Crucifixion reveals what God is like, then our entire picture of divinity must change. The pagan imagination envisioned gods who demanded offerings to appease their moods. The philosophers spoke of an Unmoved Mover, distant and untouched. But on Calvary, the true God moves. He does not receive a sacrifice — He becomes it. The Almighty bleeds, the Infinite suffers, the Immortal dies.

This overturns religion as the world has known it. Every altar before Calvary was humanity's attempt to reach upward; the Cross is God's descent downward. Every religion has a concept of sacrifice, but only Christianity reveals a God who sacrifices Himself. This is not divine cruelty but divine self-disclosure. Love shows itself not in comfort but in cost.

Saint Gregory Nazianzen once wrote, "What was not assumed was not healed." That principle, born from reflection on the Incarnation, reaches its climax on the Cross. Humanity's entire wound — physical, emotional, spiritual — is assumed into God. Pain, fear, betrayal, abandonment, even death itself are gathered into the divine experience so that nothing remains untouched by grace. There is no corner of human misery where Christ has not stood. That is why the Cross, for all its horror, radiates consolation.

The paradox is almost unbearable: the very moment when God seems most absent is the moment He is most present. "My God, My God, why have You forsaken Me?" — the cry of desolation becomes the bridge for our reconciliation. Jesus does not lose the Father; He carries our lostness into the heart of the Trinity. The silence that follows is not divine indifference but divine intimacy too deep for words.

Theologians describe this moment as *kenosis* — self-emptying. The eternal Son pours Himself out, holding nothing back. But this self-emptying is not negation; it is revelation. The Cross shows what divinity truly is: love that keeps nothing for itself. God's glory, it turns out, is His humility.

That humility changes everything we think about power. The Roman world worshipped strength. Caesar's image adorned coins, temples, banners — power meant domination. The Cross dismantled that myth forever. True power is not the ability to crush; it is the ability to endure for the sake of another. Love has its own omnipotence, and the Cross is its demonstration. The nails did not hold Christ to the wood — love did.

This is why the early Church could call Good Friday "good." The worst act in human history became the greatest revelation of God's heart. Sin reached its most violent expression, and love met it without flinching. The Cross is not an accident permitted by God; it is the moment when evil exhausts itself and collapses against infinite mercy.

Look closely at the scene again. The sky darkens. The crowd jeers. The disciples flee. Only a few remain — His mother, John, and a handful of women. To the world, it appears God has failed. But the Gospel invites us to see deeper. That apparent failure is the world's salvation unfolding in real time. Every mocking voice, every lash, every nail becomes a tool in the hand of grace. Nothing is wasted. Even hatred becomes the raw material of redemption.

In that light, the Cross becomes the answer not only to sin but to suffering itself. The problem of evil — the philosopher's greatest challenge to faith — is answered not by argument but by solidarity. God does not explain suffering; He shares it. He does not remove pain; He redeems it from within. The Crucified One does not promise an escape from the world's agony; He promises His presence in it.

This changes how Christians face pain. The believer does not deny it, nor does he seek it; he transforms it. The Cross is not a symbol of masochism but of meaning. Every act of endurance done in love becomes participation in redemption. A parent caring for a dying child, a prisoner forgiving his captor, a patient offering pain for others — these are the Cross continued in time.

The saints saw this clearly. Teresa of Ávila wrote, "In the Cross is life, and in the Cross is light." John Paul II called suffering "the place where love proves itself." When love refuses to stop loving, even when wounded, it becomes divine. The Cross is not merely something Christ did; it is the pattern by which we are remade.

And yet, that transformation would remain unfinished without what came next. The Cross without the Resurrection would be a monument to loss, not salvation. The Resurrection is the Father's "Amen" to the Son's "It is finished." It is not an afterthought but the consequence of love carried to its limit. Death, having swallowed Love, finds itself destroyed from within.

In rising, Christ does not undo the Cross; He transfigures it. The same wounds that killed now shine. The same body once broken becomes the bread of eternal life. The Cross becomes a doorway, not a dead end. "Death is swallowed up in victory," Paul exclaims, quoting Isaiah. The Resurrection proves that justice has been satisfied, mercy has triumphed, and love has the last word.

That is why Christian hope is not optimism. Optimism depends on circumstances; hope depends on resurrection. The Cross tells us that God can bring life from death, meaning from loss, beauty from ruin. If He can transform Calvary into salvation, there is nothing in our lives He cannot redeem.

In this sense, the Cross is the key to reality. It reveals the structure of existence itself: life through death, victory through surrender, exaltation through humility. Every seed that falls into the ground and dies to bear fruit, every act of generosity that costs something, every forgiveness that feels like death — all of them echo Calvary. The universe is cruciform because it was made by cruciform love.

And this is not mere poetry. It is the deepest metaphysical truth Christianity offers: love is the final law of the cosmos. The Cross is not sentimental decoration for religion; it is the pattern of creation and redemption alike. The same God who created by self-giving continues to re-create by the same act. The Cross reveals that existence itself is relational, that being and love are inseparable.

That is why the saints could say, "In the Cross is joy." They were not romanticizing pain; they were recognizing the shape of reality. Once you know that love wins through giving, every loss becomes potential glory. Calvary is not just the world's redemption; it is its revelation.

If the Cross is the pattern of reality, then every life must eventually confront it. The Cross is not something that happened to *Jesus* only; it is what happens whenever love meets a fallen world. That is why Christ does not merely invite us to admire His Cross but to carry our own. "If anyone would come after Me, let him deny himself, take up his cross, and follow Me." The words are not a threat but a promise. To share His Cross is to share His victory.

At first, that seems impossible. We recoil from suffering, from surrender, from anything that strips our illusion of control. But the paradox is that only when the ego dies can the soul breathe. The Cross is the death of self-worship — the collapse of the idol called "me." And in that collapse, freedom begins. The God who lost everything on Calvary teaches us that what we cling to most tightly is often what keeps us from joy.

To take up our cross, then, is not morbid resignation. It is an act of trust — the belief that dying to ourselves will lead to life. This is the heartbeat of discipleship. When we forgive instead of retaliate, when we serve instead of dominate, when we love without demanding return, we are already walking the hill of Golgotha in miniature. And each step loosens the chains of sin a little more.

The saints have always understood this. Francis of Assisi, who prayed to know "perfect joy," found it not in success or praise but in humiliation. He rejoiced when rejected, because he saw in that rejection the mark of his Beloved. Mother Teresa, amid decades of interior darkness, carried the Cross daily, hidden behind her smile. She said, "When you look at the Cross, you understand how much Jesus loved you. When you look at the Eucharist, you understand how much He loves you now."

These lives are not exceptions; they are blueprints. The Christian is not called to comfort but to communion — and communion always involves the Cross. The world tells us to avoid pain at all costs; the Gospel teaches us to transform it. The Cross does not glorify suffering but redeems it, turning curse into cure. Pain, when united to love, becomes fertile.

Yet this truth must be protected from distortion. Christianity does not sanctify cruelty or invite passivity in the face of injustice. Christ did not seek the Cross for its own sake; He endured it for love's sake. The goal is not pain, but participation in divine charity. To bear the Cross is not to accept abuse but to answer evil with good. The Cross is not fatalism — it is defiance: the refusal to let hate have the last word.

That defiance is cosmic. At Calvary, the battle is not simply between good and evil but between two definitions of power. One seeks to control; the other seeks to give. The first builds empires; the second builds saints. When Jesus refuses the taunts — "Come down from the Cross if you are the Son of God!" — He is not proving weakness but redefining strength. He will not come down because divine power never abandons love.

In that moment, the world sees a man dying and mocks. Heaven sees God reigning. The Cross is His throne, the nails His sceptre, the thorns His crown. Every symbol of humiliation becomes its opposite. The irony is staggering: those who mocked Him as King spoke truer than they knew. Here, enthroned in agony, He governs the universe through mercy.

That is the great reversal Christianity introduces to history. The Cross dethrones violence as the engine of meaning. Before Christ, might made right; after Christ, only love does. The Crucified becomes the standard of justice. Every time the innocent suffer, the Cross stands beside them as witness and protest. "Whatever you do to the least of these, you do to Me." The world cannot undo that identification. God has tied Himself forever to the oppressed.

This is why the Cross remains relevant in every age. It speaks to victims and perpetrators alike. To the victim, it says: your pain is not meaningless. The God who loves you has entered it. To the sinner, it says: your guilt need not define you. The price is already paid. To the sceptic, it says: here is proof of divine sincerity — a God who does not stand above suffering but shoulders it.

The philosopher Nietzsche once mocked Christianity as "a religion for the weak." In a sense, he was right — and that is its genius. It is for the weak because it is for the real. Everyone is weak when stripped of illusion, when facing death, grief, or guilt. The Cross offers not escapism but companionship in that weakness. It is the end of pretending to be gods and the beginning of learning to be beloved.

For all its apparent darkness, the Cross shines brightest where human strength fails. Its meaning is grasped not through argument but through surrender. At the end of every human solution stands this timbered paradox: the God who saves not by taking pain away, but by taking it up.

That's why the Cross is the Church's most dangerous symbol. It cannot be domesticated. You can hang it on a wall or wear it around your neck, but it will still whisper rebellion against selfishness. It exposes hypocrisy, humbles pride, and calls every soul to account. It asks not for admiration but allegiance. To look at the Crucified and remain unchanged is impossible.

The Cross divides history and humanity, yet it unites heaven and earth. It stands as the one intersection where everything converges — sin and salvation, death and life, time and eternity. It is the wound in history through which grace pours forever. Every prayer, every sacrament, every act of mercy flows from its heart. The Church does not merely remember Calvary; she lives from it.

And that life is victorious. The Resurrection does not cancel the Cross; it crowns it. The Lamb who was slain now reigns. His wounds, still visible, are the badges of love's triumph. In heaven, there are no more scars except His, because His contain the healing of all others.

When we contemplate those wounds, we glimpse our destiny. The Cross does not end in despair but in glory. "If we have died with Him," says Paul, "we shall also live with Him." Death, once the tyrant, becomes servant. Pain, once the curse, becomes passage. Love has rewritten the script of mortality.

To believe this is to live differently. Fear loses its grip. Suffering becomes bearable. Even the smallest act of love gains eternal weight. The Cross means nothing is wasted—not one tear, not one sacrifice, not one loss offered to God. Everything surrendered is stored, transfigured, redeemed.

The Cross is therefore not only an event in the past but a presence in every moment. It stands wherever a person chooses love over hatred, truth over comfort, mercy over indifference. It is the world's ongoing hinge—the place where eternity keeps touching time.

This is why the Christian faith is not a theory of morality but a story of transformation. It does not ask us merely to imitate a hero; it invites us to live in Him who died and rose. The Cross is the doorway into that life. When we pass through it, our own pain, guilt, and weakness are caught up in His and changed. "Whoever is in Christ," says Paul, "is a new creation."

That new creation is not yet visible in full. The wounds of the world remain open; injustice persists; death still stalks every life. Yet the Cross tells us that the end has already been decided. Evil is not erased yet, but it is disarmed. The serpent's fangs remain, but its venom has been neutralized. Every sorrow now carries resurrection in its seed.

This is the meaning of Christian hope. It is not naïve belief that things will work out, but the conviction that God has already worked them out. The Cross and Resurrection mean that love has already won, even if history has not yet caught up. When the world looks darkest, that truth steadies the heart. We do not hope *for* victory; we hope *from* it.

Because of the Cross, every human story can be rewritten. The thief who dies beside Christ becomes the first saint of the new covenant. A Roman soldier, hardened executioner, becomes the first evangelist, crying, "Truly this was the Son of God." The failures of Peter, the skepticism of Thomas, the persecution of Paul—all are folded into redemption. The Cross is so powerful that even its enemies become its witnesses.

For two millennia, it has continued to do the same. Empires have fallen; ideologies have risen and burned out; yet this single symbol endures, planted in every culture and age. It has adorned cathedrals and prison walls, the necks of queens and the graves of the poor. Wherever it stands, it tells the same truth: here, love paid the price—and won.

But the Cross does not merely tell us *that* we are loved; it tells us *how* we are to love. The pattern is given: self-gift, steadfastness, forgiveness. When Jesus said, "Father, forgive them," He wasn't only absolving His executioners; He was teaching His followers the grammar of heaven. To forgive those who wound you is to prove you belong to Him. To serve without applause, to sacrifice without bitterness, to endure without despair—these are the daily crucifixions by which love reigns.

In this light, every vocation becomes a share in the Cross. The mother who wakes through the night for her child, the doctor who stays in the ward long after exhaustion, the priest who prays over the dying, the worker who endures injustice without hatred—all of them, knowingly or not, participate in redemption's rhythm. The Cross is not confined to Calvary; it is scattered across the earth in quiet acts of fidelity.

And yet, these small crosses draw their meaning only from the great one. Without Christ, suffering is absurd; with Him, it becomes seed. The Cross teaches that our pain, joined to His, can bear eternal fruit. This is what it means to "offer it up": not to pretend suffering is good, but to let it be used for good. Every sigh becomes intercession; every loss becomes offering. Grace wastes nothing.

This transforms even death. The world sees death as final defeat; the Christian sees it as completion. The Cross has turned the grave into a door. "For me to live is Christ, and to die is gain." The believer who dies in faith is not extinguished but gathered—his life hidden now in the wounds of the Redeemer. The blood that redeemed the world still marks the soul that trusts in it.

All of this leads to the moment the world still cannot explain: the empty tomb. The Cross and Resurrection are one act, two movements of a single symphony. The death was love proving itself; the Resurrection was love vindicated. The same hands that were pierced now break bread. The same voice that cried "It is finished" now calls Mary by name. Sin is paid for; death is undone; and the world's end has already begun.

If this is true—and Christians dare to stake their souls on it—then every claim of the Gospel follows. There is one Mediator, because there is only one who died and rose again. There is one way to the Father, because only one has crossed the chasm. The exclusivity of the Cross is not exclusion but inclusion at the highest possible cost. The arms of Jesus are nailed open, not closed.

This is why the Cross is the only answer that satisfies both reason and the heart. It does not deny the world's pain, nor despair of it. It affirms both justice and mercy. It answers the question, "Why must there be suffering?" with a person: *Because love would not stay away.*

Here lies the heart of Christianity: God does not demand blood from humanity; He gives His own. He does not wait for our ascent; He descends. He does not forgive by decree; He forgives by dying. The Cross reveals that divine love is not sentiment but solidarity — a love that enters the worst of what we are and remains until it becomes new.

And so the Christian stands before the Cross not as spectator but as participant. To look upon it is to recognize both guilt and grace. It exposes our sin and heals it in the same gaze. It tells us that we are more lost than we admit, and more loved than we can imagine.

When all else fails—when logic breaks, when prayers falter, when pain has no explanation—the Cross remains. It is the proof that God's silence is never absence and His mercy never ends.

At the end of time, the vision of Revelation shows the Lamb "standing as though slain." The wounds are still there, but they shine. The Cross has become the throne. From it flows a river of life, watering the new creation. That is the final word on history: the sign of execution turned into the emblem of eternity.

Until that day, the Cross continues to mark us — on our foreheads at Baptism, on our bodies in prayer, on our graves in hope. It remains the sign of what God has done and the promise of what He will yet do.

The Cross is the price of love, yes—but also its victory.

It is the world's contradiction and its completion.

It is the wound through which grace entered creation, and the bridge by which creation returns to its Maker.

All roads to God begin and end here, at this wooden intersection of mercy and truth.

5

The Only Mediator: One Bridge for All

The most offensive sentence ever spoken was also the truest: "No one comes to the Father except through Me."

Modern ears hear arrogance; the early Church heard rescue. Jesus' words did not create exclusion—they exposed reality. If there is only one God, there can be only one bridge between Him and a fallen race. The claim is not tribal pride but physics of the soul. A broken creature cannot reconnect itself to the Infinite; the Infinite must cross the gap Himself.

The world's religions were built on that ache to reach across. Altars, prayers, sacrifices, and philosophies all confess the same wound: man separated from what he was made for. Every temple is a cry, every law code a reaching hand. But a cry cannot heal, and a hand cannot touch what it cannot reach. Humanity may sense God, describe His shadow, even glimpse His fingerprints, but no one can raise the dead by sincerity. If the problem were ignorance, prophets would have been enough. If it were behaviour, moral reformers could fix it. But the human problem is death—separation from the Source of life—and only the Author of life can reverse that.

We call that reversal *mediation*. A mediator joins what is divided. Yet between God and man lies an abyss no creature can cross. Philosophy can argue, ritual can plead, sacrifice can symbolise—but the gap remains. "There is one God," wrote Paul, "and one Mediator between God and men, the man Christ Jesus." His sentence is not a slogan; it is a statement of ontological necessity. One God, one race, therefore one bridge. Multiplicity would mean confusion, contradiction, and chaos. Truth, like light, can be refracted but never divided.

That is why Christianity's claim is not that it is *better* than other religions, but that it is *real*. It is not a viewpoint but an event—God becoming man. If that happened, it rewrote reality itself. Everything else is commentary. If it did not, then Christianity collapses with the rest, and humanity remains stranded. But if God truly entered flesh, died, and rose, then there exists in the universe a living pathway from death to life, and it bears a name.

Our age despises that sort of certainty. We prefer to imagine spirituality as a mountain with many trails leading upward. The picture sounds generous, but it smuggles in a fatal assumption: that humans can climb. Scripture says otherwise. The mountain is sheer rock and we are dust. Even the holiest prophet slips. Only one path reaches the summit because only one begins there and descends. All other religions are human ascent; Christianity is divine descent. Every faith tells man how to reach God; the Gospel tells how God reached man.

The first believers understood that shock. They were not marketing a new creed to compete in the religious marketplace of the empire. They were declaring that the impossible had happened—heaven invaded earth. Jesus' resurrection was not a mystical metaphor but the public proof that the bridge had been built. They did not argue that Christ was *a* way among others; they announced that the others were gone, obsolete, because the real thing had arrived. When sunlight rises, candles are still candles, but they no longer guide ships.

That conviction made the Church unstoppable. It was not the

promise of moral improvement that converted nations, but the proclamation of an event: a man who claimed to forgive sins was executed, then walked out of His tomb. Once that was believed, the question of religious choice ended. Either the claim was false, or every rival altar was empty. "If Christ has not been raised," wrote Paul, "your faith is futile." The inverse is also true: if He has been raised, every other faith built on mortal founders is futile.

This is why the apostles were hated. Empires tolerate diversity but not ultimacy. Rome could host Jupiter, Isis, and Mithras side by side because each stayed in its lane. Christianity refused. It claimed all truth as Christ's truth and all salvation as His work. That conviction still divides the world. The modern age dresses tolerance in moral language, but underneath is the same ancient demand: bow to plurality or die to relevance. Yet truth cannot share a throne. Either Jesus Christ is the one Mediator, or He is none. Either the Cross and Resurrection are the hinge of history, or they are delusion. If they are real, then every other system—religious, moral, or philosophical—is an echo without the source.

The paradox of one way is therefore not cruelty but mercy. To claim many paths is to lie about the wound. If there were other cures, the Cross would be an obscenity, God's greatest cruelty instead of His greatest love. But the crucifixion means the wound was terminal and required divine blood. The exclusivity of Christ is not narrowness; it is necessity. A surgeon is not "exclusive" for using the only instrument that saves; he is merciful for using it at all.

So the Gospel begins here: one God, one human race, one Mediator. The bridge has been lowered from heaven to earth. No one is barred from crossing except by refusal to step on it. The path is singular, but its invitation universal. The narrowness of the gate is the width of a human heart—wide enough for the world.

To understand why Christ alone can mediate between God and man, we must first understand what that mediation means. The word is simple: a mediator is one who joins what is divided. The need for one reveals the reality of separation. Humanity's tragedy is not ignorance—it is rupture. Sin is not a list of infractions; it is a broken relationship, a tearing of being itself. The creature made for communion with its Maker tried to exist without Him, and the result was death. Every religion is an attempt to mend that tear, to rebuild the bridge. But how does dust repair itself to divinity? The chasm is not moral distance; it is ontological—between what *is* and the One who *is Being itself.*

If we were merely lost travellers, we could ask for directions. If we were merely guilty, we could seek pardon. But we are dead in spirit, and dead men cannot negotiate peace. We needed not advice but resurrection. That is why no prophet, sage, or founder of another religion could be enough. They may have spoken truth, but they remained on our side of the divide. Their words could describe God, but not deliver Him. Only One who stood on both sides at once could join them—the God who became man.

This is the heart of Christian revelation. In Jesus Christ, divinity and humanity are united in one person. Not mixed, not confused, but joined without division. If He were only a man speaking for God, He could offer words but not life. If He were only God appearing to man, He could dazzle but not redeem. But as both, He becomes the living bridge—God's voice and man's answer in one heartbeat. The Cross is not a symbol of failed rebellion; it is the hinge of history where infinity touched flesh and the current of life began to flow again.

Philosophers through the ages have dreamed of climbing to heaven by reason. Mystics have tried by inner vision. Moralists have tried by discipline. All have failed for the same reason: they begin from the wrong side. You cannot climb out of a grave. The logic of mediation starts with a simple question—who can cross the gap? A being less than God cannot reach up; a being less than man cannot represent us.

Only one who is both can stand in the middle and hold both hands.

This is what Saint Paul means when he says there is one Mediator. It is not a title of honour but of function. Jesus is not a third party between rivals; He is the very place where the two meet. Think of it as the point where two circles overlap—the divine and the human intersecting in one Person. In Him, God's justice and man's need collide and reconcile. There is no second intersection, no alternate geometry of salvation. Any other system that denies this union leaves the lines forever apart.

The Incarnation, then, is not a theological curiosity; it is the structural necessity of redemption. Without it, the Cross is cruelty and the Resurrection fantasy. With it, they become the machinery of love. The Word became flesh not to offer a new philosophy but to restore being itself. The chasm was not filled by effort but by presence. God did not shout from across the canyon; He built Himself into the bridge. Every plank of that bridge is wood from His Cross, every bolt His wounds.

This is why Christianity cannot reduce itself to moral teaching or inspiration. Every religion can teach virtue; only Christ can make men new. The mediator is not a messenger delivering terms but a surgeon transplanting life. Through Him, God's grace enters humanity like oxygen into lungs. It is not metaphorical breath—it is being remade. Without Him, even the best human goodness is a corpse politely dressed.

Modern thought recoils from this logic because it removes our pride. It says plainly that the human race cannot save itself, not even its saints and sages. The cross of Christ stands as the world's verdict on self-redemption. All our efforts end in exhaustion. The tower we tried to build—Babel's echo—collapses under its own ambition. Grace must descend. The mediator must come from heaven down, not earth up.

Here lies the great reversal: we are not saved by climbing but by kneeling. Faith is not effort rewarded but surrender accepted. That is why Christianity, though accused of arrogance, is the most humbling creed on earth. It denies every human boast. It declares that no religion, no ritual, no philosophy, no moral system can reach the Father—only the Son who was sent. That truth offends, because it leaves no room for competition. But it also comforts, because it means salvation does not depend on our success. The bridge does not sway with our weight; it is anchored in God Himself.

Jesus stands in that middle place eternally—the God-man, priest and victim, offering humanity back to the Father through His own body. In Him, heaven and earth meet and kiss. The mediation is not metaphorical; it is living and ongoing. Every time a sinner is forgiven, that bridge carries the mercy across. Every time a soul rises from despair to faith, the same hands that were pierced are drawing it upward. The one Mediator still mediates.

The world calls that exclusivity; heaven calls it truth. The path is narrow because reality is singular. One God, one human nature, one Redeemer who holds both without collapse. The Cross is the centre of that reality—the point where all roads end or begin. Everything that refuses it, however noble, ends in silence. Everything that accepts it enters life.

Everything hinges on who Jesus is. If He were merely a prophet, His words might enlighten but not redeem. If He were only a moral teacher, He could inspire but not forgive. The world has had many teachers, and they have all died. Christ is different because He is not only *from* God but *of* God—"the Word made flesh, who dwelt among us." In Him, two natures meet: divine and human, whole and entire, without confusion or dilution. He is not half of each but fully both. That union is the reason there can be only one Mediator—because only in Him do the separated halves of reality meet.

The Church has spent centuries defending that mystery. Every heresy has tried to make Jesus easier to understand by trimming one side of His identity. Some made Him a god wearing a human mask; others made Him a holy man adopted by God. Both errors destroy the bridge. If He only *appeared* human, then He did not truly bear our nature or our sin. If He was merely human and later "anointed," then God never truly joined us—He only visited. But the truth confessed by the early Church and sealed by martyrs is stubborn: in the womb of Mary, God and man were fused forever. The infinite entered finitude without ceasing to be infinite; the Creator stepped into creation without abandoning heaven.

That union is not an optional doctrine; it is the engine of salvation. The Cross only saves because of who hangs on it. If Jesus were not fully divine, His death would be tragic but powerless. If He were not fully human, His death would be divine spectacle, not representation. But because He is both, His sacrifice counts for both: God offering Himself, man offering perfect obedience. The nails that held Him held together heaven and earth. "In Christ," wrote Paul, "God was reconciling the world to Himself." Those words are not poetry—they are mechanics. The repair of the universe required the Carpenter Himself.

Imagine two realms separated by an abyss. If you stretch a rope from one side only, it dangles into emptiness. To bridge the gap, both ends must be fixed. The Incarnation is God tying one end to heaven and the other to earth within a single Person. From that point onward, humanity has an anchor within divinity. The Son became what we are so that we might share what He is. Salvation is not escape from humanity but the glorification of it—the human taken up into God's own life without being erased. That is what "deification" means: not becoming gods by nature, but participating in God by grace.

This explains why every alternative fails. Other religions begin with man reaching upward; Christianity begins with God descending. The difference is not degree but kind. The gap between finite and infinite is unbridgeable from below. No prophet, however holy, could speak divinity into humanity. No moral effort can recreate innocence. Philosophy can polish thought but cannot cleanse guilt. The Mediator must contain both worlds in Himself. That is why Christ is not merely *a* teacher of truth—He is the Truth. Not a revealer of life—He *is* Life. Words and rituals point to what He *is*.

When the apostles met the risen Jesus, they did not just see proof that He lived; they saw what humanity was meant to become. He was still recognisably Himself—He ate, He spoke, He bore wounds—but transfigured. The union of God and man was complete, and human nature itself had been carried into eternity. In Him, we glimpse our own destiny: to share in divine life, not as spectators but participants. That is mediation fulfilled—creation reconnected to its Source, not by philosophy but by Person.

The world, however, still tries to separate what God has joined. Some prefer a Jesus of moral ideals, stripped of divinity—safe, admirable, non-threatening. Others prefer a mystical Christ who never really took on the grime of flesh, a spirit-guide floating above history. Both are comfortable lies. The first keeps us in charge; the second keeps us untouched. The real Christ destroys both illusions. He is the God who sweated, bled, and wept—and the man who raised the dead. He claims everything human and heals it by joining it to everything divine.

This is the meaning behind the ancient formula of the Council of Chalcedon: one and the same Christ, the Son, perfect in divinity and perfect in humanity, truly God and truly man, of one substance with the Father and one with us, united "without confusion, change, division, or separation." Those old words are not theological furniture; they are the guardrails of salvation. Remove them, and the bridge collapses. Keep them, and you have the only structure that spans eternity and time.

When Jesus prayed, He spoke as man to the Father. When He healed,

He acted as God. When He suffered, He did so as man. When He forgave, He did so as God. In every gesture, the two natures worked in harmony—never mixed, never apart. His human lips pronounced divine pardon; His divine power worked through human touch. The Mediator lived every second as the intersection of heaven and earth.

This is why He could say, without madness or metaphor, "He who has seen Me has seen the Father." No prophet ever dared that. Moses saw God's back; Isaiah saw His train; Muhammad claimed His message; the Buddha sought dissolution. Only Christ revealed God's face, because only Christ *is* that face. To see Him is to encounter the uncreated clothed in created form. To hear Him is to hear the eternal Word speaking our language.

In Jesus, the question "Where is God?" receives its final answer. Not in an idea, not in a temple, not in an unreachable sky—but in a Person. The divine nature did not visit humanity for a season; it married it. The Incarnation is permanent. The Word made flesh remains flesh, now glorified. The Mediator lives forever because the union He forged can never be undone. Heaven and earth are welded together in Him, and that weld is eternal.

That is why salvation cannot be duplicated. To suggest another mediator is to imply another Incarnation, another Cross, another Resurrection. There can be none. God has already entered history once for all. The bridge stands finished. The only question left is whether we will walk across.

Picture two cliffs facing each other across a bottomless gulf. One side is God's holiness—perfect, blazing, untouchable. The other is man—finite, broken, guilty. Every religion has tried to throw something across that canyon: good deeds, prayers, philosophies, mystical experiences. All collapse before they reach the other side. The gap isn't spatial but moral and metaphysical. It isn't a few metres— it's infinity. Humanity cannot reach the Infinite any more than a candle can leap into the sun. For centuries we've been building scaffolds of good intention, climbing until the beams tremble, and then wondering why we fall. The problem isn't effort. The problem is direction. We keep building up; God alone can build across.

The gospel begins with that reversal. The bridge of salvation is not constructed from the human shore but from the divine. It descends like lightning, not ascends like smoke. "No one has ascended into heaven except the One who descended from heaven, the Son of Man." Every other religion begins with man searching for God. Christianity begins with God searching for man. All other faiths are maps drawn from below; the Gospel is God's descent into the maze with us. The entire story of Scripture—from Eden to Bethlehem, from Bethlehem to Calvary—is the record of God crossing the distance man could not.

Think of Jacob's ladder. He saw angels ascending and descending between heaven and earth, but the top of the ladder stood not on human ground—it reached into heaven because God lowered it. That vision foreshadowed Christ. He is the ladder, the bridge, the stairway by which heaven touches earth. Every rung is His humility: birth, suffering, death, resurrection, glory. We climb only because He stooped. The Incarnation is not sentimental divine empathy; it is architecture—the engineering of redemption. The foundation is God's initiative; the support beams are His obedience; the span is His flesh.

That descent runs through the whole Gospel. God speaks the universe into existence by His Word, then speaks that Word again into a virgin's womb. The infinite becomes infant, the Creator now crying in a manger. Heaven's throne becomes a feed trough. Angels who had sung His glory now watch shepherds kneel before Him. This is the mystery of condescension—not humiliation, but self-giving. God stoops without ceasing to be God. He enters His creation not as conqueror but carpenter. He eats our food, bears our weariness, weeps at our graves. He takes on not just our skin but our story. Every hunger, every temptation, every ache of loneliness is now familiar to the Almighty.

That is how the bridge was built. From our side, it looked like failure. A penniless rabbi from a backwater province dies on a Roman cross—how could that be God? Yet from heaven's side, the beams were locking into place. The wood of the manger became the wood of the Cross, and the bridge was complete. The carpenter of Nazareth had finished His work. When He cried, "It is finished," He wasn't announcing defeat; He was announcing structural integrity. The gulf was spanned. Humanity had, for the first time since Eden, a road home.

This explains why the direction of grace is always downward. We don't ascend to God by intelligence or virtue; He descends to us in mercy. "God opposes the proud but gives grace to the humble." Pride builds ladders that reach nowhere. Humility kneels and finds God already beside it. The entire drama of salvation is this paradox: the Infinite bends down, and by bending, lifts the finite up. We don't conquer heaven; we are carried there on the shoulders of the Son.

That descent also answers the illusion of spiritual competition. Many imagine all faiths as mountain paths winding upward, some steeper, some easier, all converging near the summit. But that image is upside down. Humanity is not climbing a mountain toward God; it's trapped in a pit, calling upward. There are no paths that reach the summit from below. Only one rope has been dropped, and it is Christ Himself. To grab another is to grasp air. His exclusivity is not arrogance; it is realism. Only one bridge exists because only one God became man.

Once you see that, the word "tolerance" loses its glamour. It sounds noble, but it assumes that all ideas about God are equally partial glimpses of a truth too vast to grasp. Yet if God has revealed Himself fully in Christ, partial glimpses are no longer enough. The light has come. To treat the incarnation as one myth among others is not generous—it is blind. The sun does not compete with candles. When truth has walked among us, to pretend uncertainty is not humility; it's denial.

Christ's descent also dismantles the pride of religion itself. The point of the bridge is to remove boasting. No man can claim, "I have climbed." Every believer stands at the same level—sinners carried by grace. That is why Christianity can be both utterly exclusive in truth and utterly inclusive in invitation. The path is one, but it's open to all. Jew or Gentile, scholar or slave, saint or criminal—all must cross the same span, and all are welcome. The bridge was built wide enough for the world.

The tragedy is not that the bridge is narrow but that so many refuse to step on it. Humanity still insists on building from its own side—still hammering moral planks and philosophical ropes that always snap. Yet the real bridge stands ready. God has already done the impossible. To reject it is not to choose another valid path; it is to choose the abyss. The gulf of sin remains open for those who will not cross by grace. God will not force our feet; love never coerces. But the invitation remains: "Come to Me, all who labour and are heavy-laden, and I will give you rest." He does not ask for perfection, only surrender.

So the logic of the Gospel is simple and humbling. Salvation comes down, not up. Heaven's builder has finished His work. The bridge stands from eternity into time, from holiness into flesh, from death into life. All other roads lead only to the edge. Here alone the chasm closes. Here alone, the wanderer can finally walk home.

Sin is not an opinion. It is a condition—something wrong at the root of human life, not merely at the edges. You can feel it even if you do not believe in Scripture: the restlessness, the guilt that no therapy can fully quiet, the lurking certainty that death is more than biology; it is judgment. Humanity suffers from one sickness, and that sickness is separation from God. It is the wound of the soul torn away from its Source, like a branch snapped from the tree that feeds it. The branch still looks alive for a while, but its greenness is borrowed time. Every grave on earth is proof of that separation. Every war, every betrayal, every sleepless conscience is its symptom.

If there is one disease, there can only be one cure. And that cure must correspond exactly to the poison that caused it. Doctors call this the "law of likeness": the antidote must meet the toxin on its own terms, matching it molecule for molecule. The Cross is that antidote. The infection was sin; the remedy had to reach into it and neutralize it from within. The fall happened through man; the restoration had to happen through man. But no ordinary man could withstand the full dose of evil without dying under it. Only one could: the God-man, whose divine life could absorb death itself and survive. That is why there is one Mediator—because there is one wound, one poison, one cure.

Christ's exclusivity is therefore not arrogance; it's anatomy. He alone possesses both natures necessary to heal the split: the divine to give life, the human to represent ours. Every other religious founder, however noble, was infected by the same disease he tried to cure. Muhammad, Buddha, Confucius—all died as sons of Adam, not as second Adams. They could teach about the problem, but they could not remove it. They were doctors who knew symptoms but not the medicine. Jesus is the medicine—living serum, the antidote running with the very life of God. "I am the life," He said. Not "I have it," but "I am it." That's the difference between prophet and Redeemer.

To call Him the only way, then, is not to boast in a tribe but to describe reality. You can invent new philosophies, perform rituals, chant mantras, or meditate until the self dissolves; none of it can resurrect a corpse. The human condition is death; the cure must be life Himself. Imagine a village stricken by a single plague. A scientist discovers a cure—one compound that neutralizes the disease perfectly. Would it be arrogance to say "only this medicine works"? No, it would be mercy. To offer false options would be cruelty. The paradox of the Gospel is not that there is one cure, but that God made one at all.

This also explains the universality of salvation. The same sickness affects every human being, regardless of culture, history, or creed. There is no Western sin, Eastern sin, rich sin, or poor sin. There is only human sin—alienation from God, the Author of life. Because the wound is universal, the cure must be universal. The Cross is not parochial; it is cosmic. Christ's blood does not belong to a race or a nation but to the species. "He died for all," Paul insists, and the words mean exactly what they say. There is one bridge because there is one humanity, one Mediator because there is one Creator.

This is why Christianity alone can hold together two truths the world finds irreconcilable: that God loves everyone, yet salvation is found only in Christ. The world hears contradiction; the Gospel reveals causation. Precisely because He loves everyone, God provided one way that works for everyone. Multiplicity would mean partial cures, temporary relief, incompatible chemistries of grace. Reality does not work that way. Water quenches thirst everywhere; fire burns everywhere; gravity pulls everywhere. So too grace saves everywhere—but it flows from one source.

Some people recoil at that logic, saying, "But surely sincerity must count for something." It does—but sincerity does not alter chemistry. A man who sincerely drinks poison still dies. Sincerity without truth is tragedy. Good intentions cannot turn false gods into real ones. The prophets of Israel understood that with terrifying clarity. They saw their nation burn incense to Baal and weep while doing it. Emotion did not save them; repentance did. Truth and mercy meet only in one place—on the wood where the antidote was poured out.

This is why Christianity is not pluralism with a Christian accent. It is revelation with a human face. Other faiths grope toward God; this one begins with God grasping us. Every religion shows man's fingerprints reaching upward. The Gospel shows God's hand descending. That's the difference between myth and incarnation, between philosophy and salvation. The first are shadows on the cave wall; the second is the sun stepping inside.

The "one antidote" image also defuses the charge of arrogance. When Christians say Jesus is the only way, they are not claiming superiority; they are confessing dependence. The proud man says, "I can find my own path." The Christian says, "I was dying, and He found me." There is no room for boasting in the hospital ward of grace. To accept the only cure is humility, not pride. What offends the world is not our claim to exclusive truth but its implication: that we are too sick to save ourselves. That wound to pride has always been humanity's deepest resistance to the Gospel.

But the truth stands: the Cross is the cure. The Resurrection is proof that it worked. Death itself was infected and healed from within. Humanity's bloodstream has been cleansed at its Source. That is why there can never be another Mediator—because there will never be another death like His, another blood like His, another victory like His. The antidote has been administered; the cure is complete.

Still, the world keeps swallowing substitutes: self-help, therapy without repentance, spirituality without holiness, "positive energy" instead of grace. These may numb symptoms, but the poison remains. Only one life conquers death; only one Mediator offers it freely. That is not intolerance—it is reality. The heart cannot run on wishful thinking. The soul cannot breathe false air. Life comes from the Life-giver, or it doesn't come at all.

So we return to the simplest formula of all: one disease, one cure. One race, one Redeemer. The name written on that vial of medicine is Jesus Christ, Son of God and Son of Man. Every soul that lives forever will live by that blood, whether it knew His name in this world or learned it in the next. The bridge of salvation is singular, but its span

THE ONE WAY

reaches the horizon. The antidote is one, but it is enough for all.

Human beings are incurably religious. From the first campfires of pre-history we have reached upward, sensing that the world is too ordered, too beautiful, too tragic to be an accident. That longing is the best evidence of our divine origin. Yet longing alone cannot save. Desire for truth does not equal possession of it, and worship pointed in the wrong direction cannot heal the wound between God and man. Christianity does not deny that other religions contain moments of light; it simply insists that light scattered among mirrors is not the same as the sun itself.

Islam honours one Creator, treasures moral discipline, and venerates Jesus as a prophet. Its reverence for one God preserves a fragment of the revelation given to Abraham, and its call to prayer acknowledges the Creator's sovereignty. Yet Islam stops short of the centre. It denies the Sonship of Christ and the Cross that reconciles heaven and earth, the two pillars on which redemption stands. To call Jesus only a messenger is to refuse the message made flesh. A prophet can tell us what God commands; only the Son can make us children of the Father. Without the Son there is no revelation of the Father, and without the Resurrection there is no victory over death. Islam can speak of mercy, but it cannot explain how mercy and justice meet. It points upward but cannot bridge the gulf. And without bridging that gulf, it cannot offer salvation. Its devotion is sincere and disciplined, but its theology leaves humanity alone before a distant God—Creator, yes, but not Father. The gulf remains, and without the Mediator who unites God and man, the road ends at the edge of the abyss.

Hinduism perceives a universe saturated with divinity; it senses, correctly, that the world depends on the Absolute and that behind the diversity of things lies a single source. It captures humanity's intuition that existence is sacred and that every creature bears a spark of the divine. Yet this insight slides easily toward a pantheism that borders on paganism: the belief that all things *are* God and that countless gods embody fragments of the divine whole. In that vision, Creator and creation merge, and worship multiplies across an endless pantheon. Christianity draws the opposite line. It proclaims one personal Creator distinct from His creation—transcendent, yet immanent through love. Hinduism dissolves the person into the fire; it loses the human in the process of finding the whole. Salvation becomes absorption, individuality disappears, and love—which requires a "you" and an "I"—has no place to stand. In its poetry everything becomes God and nothing remains human. Christianity sees a higher miracle: the Creator and the creature meeting without confusion, the finite lifted into the infinite yet remaining itself. Love requires two, and the Hindu vision loses the Lover and the beloved. The Gospel keeps both and joins them forever in Christ. In Him, union is communion, not dissolution; participation, not extinction. The divine life shared with humanity does not erase the human but perfects it, so that the redeemed remain truly themselves while shining with God's glory.

Buddhism begins with a piercing insight—suffering marks all life. It faces the human condition with honesty and compassion. But its cure is silence: to extinguish desire, to let the self fade into nothingness. It diagnoses the pain but mistakes its cause. Suffering is not the consequence of existence but of alienation from its Source. The Christian agrees that desire turned inward enslaves, but desire turned toward God redeems. The answer is not the extinction of longing but its fulfilment in love. The Buddha offered detachment from the wheel; Christ shattered the wheel itself. He entered suffering, carried it, and transfigured it into glory. On the Cross He showed that pain can be turned into offering, not merely endured or escaped. Buddhism teaches compassion as a discipline; Christianity reveals compassion as a Person who dies for His enemies. Enlightenment promises escape; resurrection promises transformation. One teaches peace by withdrawal, the other offers peace through union with the Living God. Compassion alone cannot save; only a Redeemer who conquers death can.

Post-Temple Judaism still guards the revelation of the one true God, the moral law, and the prophetic vision of justice. It remains a living testimony to God's election of Israel and His faithfulness through exile and return. Yet the story pauses before its climax. The sacrifices have ceased, the altar stands empty, and the promise spoken through the prophets waits for recognition of its fulfilment. The Messiah has come, but His people did not know Him. Christianity does not despise its mother faith; it honours her for giving the world the Scriptures, the covenants, and the Christ Himself. But it mourns that the curtain of the Temple was torn and still so many wait outside. The covenant was not abolished but completed in the Lamb whose blood sealed it forever. The prophets' words—about a suffering servant, a new heart, and God dwelling among His people—have all been realised in Jesus. The tragedy is not rejection alone but incompletion: the melody began by Abraham and Moses resolves in Christ, yet much of Israel still sings without hearing the final chord.

Each of these traditions holds some echo of truth, and those echoes matter. Conscience, natural law, and glimpses of the divine are real signposts left by God in every heart. They prove that the human race has not forgotten entirely how to pray. Yet signposts are not destinations. None of these systems can remove guilt, heal death, or unite humanity to the living God. They are human searchlights sweeping a dark sky. Christianity announces that the dawn has broken.

This does not make the Christian claim arrogant; it makes it accountable. To confess that Jesus is the only way is to say that no human scheme—religious, philosophical, or moral—can climb out of the grave. A prophet can tell the truth; only God can make truth alive. A law can restrain evil; only grace can transform it. Meditation can quiet the mind; only the Spirit can recreate the heart. The limits of every other path reveal what the Gospel supplies: the actual presence of God in human flesh and the power of His Resurrection.

The Church therefore sees in other faiths both beauty and tragedy—beauty because the human soul still reaches for its Maker, tragedy because it stops short of the Cross. "What you worship as unknown," Paul told the Athenians, "this I proclaim to you." That sentence remains the Church's posture: not contempt, but completion. Christianity does not scorn the search; it declares that the search is over. The answer has a face and a name.

From this conviction flows the missionary impulse that built cathedrals and carried Scripture into every language. Christians are sent, not because others have no light at all, but because they lack the Light of the world. Every honest seeker deserves to hear that the bridge exists and that it already spans the abyss. To keep silent would not be humility but negligence. Truth shared is not domination; it is mercy.

The modern world recoils from such certainty. It prefers to flatten distinctions, to praise sincerity over accuracy. Yet sincerity cannot raise the dead. The religions of men tell us to strive upward; the Gospel tells us Someone has already descended. The others call us to effort; Christ calls us to trust. The contrast is not between good and evil religions but between human reaching and divine rescue. One begins with "try harder." The other begins with "It is finished."

The final verdict is simple. Other paths contain insight, wisdom, moral beauty, but they cannot save because they cannot change what we are. They leave the human heart under the same sentence: sin and death. Only one faith proclaims that God Himself has borne that sentence and broken it. Only one name—Jesus Christ—bridges eternity and time. The rest are lights that fade when the sun rises. The truth is not plural; it is personal. It has scars, and it is alive.

The bridge Christ built was not theory. It was hammered together in blood and verified in an empty tomb. On the Cross the Mediator did not negotiate peace between two stubborn parties; He absorbed the full consequence of separation into Himself. Justice demanded that sin be answered; mercy longed to forgive it. At Calvary those two attributes of God—often imagined as rivals—met and kissed. "He Himself bore our sins in His body on the tree," wrote Peter. In that moment the Judge and the condemned were one and the same Person. The sentence was carried out, yet love endured it. The Cross is not divine appeasement; it is divine self-giving.

Christ mediates not by speech but by substitution. Where every religion offers instruction—"do this and live"—He offers intervention: *"I will do it for you, that you may live."* He stands in the gap not as diplomat but as victim. When His arms stretched wide, they reached from God to man. Every blow of the hammer was a bolt fixing the bridge to both shores. At Golgotha the abyss closed; sin was judged and mercy released in one act. The curtain in the Temple tore because the barrier it symbolised was gone.

From that hour the relationship between God and humanity changed forever. Before the Cross, worship always looked forward—sacrifice after sacrifice, symbol after symbol. After the Cross, the symbols were fulfilled. The blood of bulls could only cover guilt; the blood of Christ removes it. Every altar since Eden had been humanity reaching upward with smoke. Calvary is God reaching downward with flame. The mediator stands not beside us pleading but within us recreating.

Yet the Cross alone would be half the story. If it ended in death, love would remain noble but defeated. The Resurrection proves that the mediation succeeded. Death entered the arena and lost. When the stone rolled away, it was not merely a corpse revived but humanity itself raised into the life of God. The same body that hung limp now breathed with uncreated energy. The same hands that bore nails now blessed creation. Jesus did not escape the tomb as an apparition; He carried human nature through death and out the other side. The bridge is not a metaphor—it is a living Man.

That risen life is the new centre of the universe. From it, a current of reconciliation flows outward. When Christ appeared to His disciples and said, "Peace be with you," He was not offering sentiment but declaring that the war was over. His wounds remained, not as evidence of defeat but as doors through which glory shines. Humanity's rebellion had pierced God; now God's love pours back through the holes we made. Every healed conscience, every forgiven sinner, every act of courage in His name is the pulse of that same victory.

The Resurrection also reveals what mediation means for time itself. It is not a past event we admire but a present reality we inhabit. The Mediator lives, and His life permeates the world through the Spirit. "Because I live, you also will live." That promise is more than comfort; it is mechanics. The Spirit applies what the Son achieved. In baptism we are joined to His death and rise in His life. In the Eucharist we feed on the same body that conquered death. Confession, anointing, marriage, ordination—all are channels of the same mediation, ways in which divine grace touches matter. Heaven's bridge does not hover above the earth; it passes through every sacrament, every act of faith, every sigh of repentance.

This is why Christianity insists that salvation is not an abstraction or moral ideal. It is participation in a Person. To be saved is to share the life of the risen Christ. Nothing less will do. Moral progress without union with Him is rehabilitation without resurrection. The Gospel does not improve the old nature; it crucifies and recreates it. The Mediator does not negotiate better terms for sinners; He turns them into sons.

The Cross and Resurrection together form one movement—descent and ascent, death and life, justice and mercy. Without Calvary, Easter would be impossible; without Easter, Calvary would be meaningless.

At the Cross God descends into our death; in the Resurrection He raises our humanity into His life. The bridge stands because both pillars hold. Every attempt to take one without the other—suffering without glory, moralism without grace, optimism without repentance—collapses back into human striving.

Through this living mediation the universe itself begins to heal. The tomb garden is the first field of the new creation. When Mary mistook the risen Jesus for a gardener, she was not entirely wrong. The Second Adam was tending Eden restored. Every redeemed soul, every act of mercy, every reconciliation is a seed from that garden. The world still groans, but its ground has been turned. The bridge has touched earth; resurrection power is already working its way through the soil of history.

The Cross was the cost; the Resurrection the receipt. Together they prove that God has not merely forgiven but transformed humanity. The Mediator does not point us to a distant paradise—He carries paradise within Himself and invites us to share it. His presence among us now is the guarantee that the bridge will one day reach its farthest shore, when death itself will be swallowed up in victory.

The Cross and the Resurrection prove that the bridge is finished. What began as a promise in a garden and was forged in blood on a hill now stretches through every century. But God's plan is never random; it follows a pattern. He starts with one to reach all. One man, one nation, one mother. The stream of grace always narrows before it widens. The covenant with Abraham was meant for every tribe; Israel's election was the doorway for the world. In Christ that doorway became a Person. The narrow path was never about exclusion—it was how mercy got to everyone.

God narrows to expand. The same pattern shapes the Church. One Body so that every person can belong to it. One Gospel so that every people can hear it. The world calls this narrow; heaven calls it simple.

THE ONLY MEDIATOR: ONE BRIDGE FOR ALL

Truth can't contradict itself. If there were many bridges, each claiming to span the same chasm, they would cancel one another. The beauty of the Gospel is its coherence: one Mediator for one humanity.

That is why the charge of intolerance misses the point. Reality is already singular. Water quenches thirst everywhere; fire burns everywhere. Life has one source, and death one cure. The claim that Christ alone saves isn't a slogan—it's the logic of creation. If He really is the Word through whom all things were made, then there can be no salvation apart from Him. To say otherwise would be to divide the universe from its own heartbeat.

The "narrow gate" that Jesus spoke about is not a barrier; it's a lifeline. A doctor who says there's one treatment for a disease isn't cruel; he's truthful. The paradox is not that there's only one medicine, but that it's offered to anyone free of charge. The Cross doesn't limit mercy; it locates it. The invitation is wide as the world, but the doorway is the same for every soul—repentance and faith in the Son who died and rose again.

The particularity of Christ also explains the wideness of His kingdom. At Pentecost the Spirit didn't erase languages; He spoke through all of them. The truth didn't flatten culture; it filled it. Each nation heard the same message in its own voice. That moment wasn't uniformity; it was harmony. The one bridge doesn't erase difference; it joins difference to its source. God's unity makes diversity safe. Without it, difference becomes division; with it, diversity becomes worship.

This is why the Church must speak. If there were many ways to the Father, silence would be kindness. But if there is only one, silence becomes betrayal. The first Christians preached because they had seen the bridge with their own eyes. They weren't selling religion; they were announcing rescue. To keep that news private would have been cruelty. The Gospel is not a ladder of virtue but a lifeline of grace. Throwing it out to others is not arrogance—it's love.

THE ONE WAY

The modern world still struggles with that simplicity. It prefers spiritual democracy—many truths, all equal, none binding. But sincerity doesn't raise the dead, and pluralism can't forgive a single sin. The Gospel is stubborn because it deals with facts, not opinions. A tomb was empty. A man who was God walked out of it. That event leaves no room for alternatives. Either it happened, or it didn't. If it did, then every road that ignores it ends at the same wall.

The Cross and the Resurrection reveal not only who God is but who we are meant to become. Through the one Mediator, humanity finally finds its purpose. Our goal isn't escape from the world but its renewal. The risen Christ is the first piece of the new creation, and He invites us to follow. Every act of forgiveness, every moment of faith, every step of courage in His name extends the bridge a little farther into the world's darkness. The Church is not a club guarding membership; it's the structure of that bridge still under construction until the last soul crosses.

And the story ends where it began—in a garden. The first garden closed because man turned inward. The new garden opened when the stone rolled away and the Gardener spoke Mary's name. In that instant, death's long rule was broken. The way back to the Father was no longer blocked by shame but paved by grace. Every believer who dies in Christ steps onto that same bridge and finds it solid beneath their feet.

So the final word of the Gospel is invitation. The bridge stands. The cure exists. The door is open. There will not be another because there doesn't need to be. One God, one Mediator, one hope. The way is single, but the welcome is endless. The gate is narrow, but the kingdom beyond it has no walls. The bridge still bears the marks of the nails—proof that love carried the weight and did not break. Step onto it, and it will hold.

6

Grace in the World: How Christ Reaches the Unreached

Every Christian eventually asks the same question: *What about the people who never heard of Jesus?*

If salvation comes through Him alone, what becomes of the millions who lived and died before His name was spoken—or who live now where His Gospel has never been preached? It is an old question, older than any missionary map. It reaches back to the first century, when the apostles began to realise that the boundaries of Israel could not contain the reach of Christ.

The New Testament never dodges that question; it answers it in two words: grace reaches. The story of salvation does not end with a sealed tomb or a closed circle of believers. It bursts outward, backward, downward. The Cross stood in time, but its power is not confined to time. If God truly became man, then His mercy can move anywhere humanity has been.

That is the meaning of one of Scripture's strangest passages—Peter's line that Christ "was put to death in the flesh but made alive in the Spirit, in which He went and preached to the spirits in prison" (1 Pet 3:18–20). The early Church called this moment the *Harrowing of Hades*.

THE ONE WAY

Between Good Friday and Easter morning, Christ descended into the realm of the dead—not to suffer, but to announce victory. The light of the Gospel reached even those who had died in shadow. The tomb became a pulpit, and the sermon was freedom.

Artists have painted the scene for centuries: the gates of the underworld blown from their hinges, Adam and Eve pulled from their graves, prophets and patriarchs rising behind them. The point is not geography but grace. If death itself cannot keep Christ out, then no human heart or culture is beyond His reach. The descent into Hades was not a footnote to Easter; it was its first mission trip.

That vision answers more than an ancient curiosity; it sets a pattern. The same grace that reached backward into the dead now reaches outward into the living. Christ does not stop at the borders of baptismal water; He goes wherever conscience and longing have left an open door. The light that broke into Hades still searches every corner of creation.

Paul says as much in his letter to the Romans: "When Gentiles, who do not have the law, do by nature what the law requires... they show that the law is written on their hearts, their conscience also bearing witness" (2:14–15). Conscience and natural law are not substitutes for revelation; they are its whispers. They are the places where prevenient grace—grace that comes *before* the Gospel is heard—begins to work. Every act of kindness, every hunger for truth, every pang of guilt is the Spirit moving a soul toward light. No one comes to the Father except through Christ, yet Christ is already seeking everyone.

This doesn't erase responsibility; it explains opportunity. Each person will be judged by the light he or she has received and by the response to it. The tribesman who never saw a Bible is not measured by what he could not know but by whether he followed the grace that reached him through conscience, creation, and moral insight. Still, that grace is always Christ's. There are not two kinds of salvation—one for the informed and another for the ignorant—but one grace applied in many ways. Every rescue, whether explicit or mysterious, flows from the same Cross.

The Church Fathers loved that image. Irenaeus called Christ "the one who becomes what we are, to make us what He is." That descent is not limited to Bethlehem or Calvary; it happens wherever the divine Word touches human dust. The Logos who entered the womb also enters history's forgotten places, the spaces where no missionary has yet arrived. Grace is not a fence around the Church but the current that carries the Church forward.

At the same time, Scripture refuses to let that truth soften the urgency of mission. That God can reach the unreached does not mean we leave them unreached. The same Paul who wrote that conscience can bear witness also spent his life crossing seas to proclaim Christ aloud. The Harrowing of Hades was God's act; evangelisation is ours. Grace can work in silence, but love compels us to speak.

The heart of Christian hope rests on this balance: God's mercy is wider than we imagine, and His way is narrower than we prefer. Everyone will meet Christ—some as Saviour, some as Judge. Those who never knew His name will discover that every moment of goodness in their lives was His hidden hand. Those who did know and refused will find that judgment is simply the truth unveiled.

The Gospel therefore invites both trust and awe. Trust, because no one slips through God's fingers by accident. Awe, because the stakes are real. The bridge is strong enough for the world, but it must be crossed. Grace moves toward every heart, but every heart must still choose what to do with it

The Gospels tell the story of Jesus' death and resurrection in earthly time, but behind that history lies a mystery that reaches into every age. Between the Friday of the Cross and the dawn of Easter, something happened that human eyes never saw. Christ entered the silence of death—not as a prisoner, but as its conqueror. The early Church called this moment *the descent into hell* or *the harrowing of Hades.* It is the first sign that grace has no borders.

Peter gives the hint: "He went and preached to the spirits in prison." The sentence is brief but explosive. The Son of God steps into the realm where no prophet, priest, or philosopher could ever go. The light of the world shines in the place of shadow. Death, which had ruled unchallenged since Adam, meets Someone it cannot contain.

The Church never imagined that descent as an extra chapter of suffering. It was victory carried to its farthest edge. In hymns and icons, Christ breaks the doors of the underworld, tramples its locks, and pulls Adam and Eve up by the wrist. Behind them follow patriarchs, prophets, and the nameless righteous of every generation. The message is not that all were saved automatically, but that the offer of salvation reached even there. No corner of creation is untouched by the Cross.

That scene answers the question every human heart asks: *Is there any place where grace cannot go?* The answer is no. If Christ descended to the dead, He can descend into any darkness. The harrowing of Hades shows that God does not rescue from a distance. He enters the place of loss to bring the lost home. Every grave dug since the beginning of the world becomes a doorway He can pass through.

It also shows that salvation is not a timeline but a reality anchored in eternity. The Cross stands in one hour of history, yet its power stretches both directions. The blood of Christ flows backward to the faithful who awaited Him and forward to the faithful who follow Him. Abraham, Moses, Ruth, Isaiah—they were not saved by a different covenant, but by the same grace delivered later on Calvary. When Christ entered the realm of the dead, He gathered them to Himself as proof that His redemption covers every age.

The descent also explains the strange peace of Holy Saturday. Between the agony of Friday and the triumph of Sunday, heaven

GRACE IN THE WORLD: HOW CHRIST REACHES THE UNREACHED

is silent but active. On the surface, the world mourns. Beneath, the Redeemer works. In that silence the earth rests while its Maker remakes it. The day between death and resurrection becomes a symbol for all the in-between places of human life—times when nothing seems to move, yet grace is tunnelling underneath.

For the Church, this event is more than history; it's a pattern of hope. Whenever we enter suffering, we walk the same descent. Christ has been there before us. In the dark nights of the soul, when prayer feels buried and faith feels like a stone, we share the Saturday between death and resurrection. The harrowing of Hades means that even there, Christ is at work. Hell itself has been invaded; despair is no longer absolute.

The Creed keeps the memory alive in one quiet line: *He descended to the dead.* It reminds us that the Gospel is not an escape from reality but its reclamation. Salvation does not float above history; it digs into its deepest layers. Grace goes lower than sin ever fell. No one will face death without meeting the One who has already passed through it.

That truth gives shape to Christian mission. We proclaim Christ not because He is confined to the Church, but because He has gone before us into every land and language. The harrowing of Hades is the first evangelisation, and every act of witness echoes it. When believers carry the Gospel into new places, they are not bringing God to where He is absent; they are unveiling the God who is already there, working beneath the surface.

The descent also guards against pride. It reminds the Church that grace is God's movement, not ours. Christ reached the dead before the apostles reached the living. He acts first; we follow. Every conversion, every awakening, every moment of repentance begins because the Spirit has already descended into that heart's hidden places and called it by name.

So the story of the harrowing is not about geography but about reach. Wherever death once ruled—whether in tombs or hearts—Christ's light now shines. He has walked the length of the shadow and left a trail of resurrection behind Him. The descent into hell is the Gospel in miniature: God goes where we cannot, and when He rises, He brings captives with Him.

The descent of Christ into death shows that grace can reach anywhere. Paul goes further: it can reach *anyone*. Even those who never heard a prophet's voice still carry, deep within, a faint echo of the Word. That echo is conscience. It is the law written on the heart.

He describes it in Romans 2: "When Gentiles, who do not have the law, do by nature what the law requires, they show that the work of the law is written on their hearts, while their conscience also bears witness." Paul is not inventing a new idea. He is naming what every person already knows—that moral awareness is built into us. Every culture on earth, however flawed, recognises some version of right and wrong: honour your parents, keep your promises, protect the innocent, do not murder. Conscience is creation's memory of its Maker.

That memory can fade but never vanish. It may be dulled by habit or twisted by fear, yet it still flickers. When a person tells the truth even at a cost, or feels shame after cruelty, or wonders if there is more to life than appetite, the Spirit is moving. Those moments are not accidents of evolution; they are grace at work before knowledge, what theologians call *prevenient grace*. God does not wait until the Gospel is preached to start speaking. He whispers through conscience long before anyone hears His name.

This is why no human being is ever entirely without revelation. Creation itself preaches. The psalmist says, "Day to day pours out speech, and night to night declares knowledge." The order of the world, the beauty of its laws, the hunger for meaning that rises in every generation—these are the first pages of Scripture written in things. Conscience reads those pages and turns them into a question: *Who made me, and what does He ask of me?* That question is the seed of faith.

Yet conscience alone cannot finish the story. It can accuse and excuse, but it cannot redeem. It can tell us we are wrong, but not make us right. Every honest soul who listens to conscience eventually runs into its limit. The law written on the heart can expose sin; it cannot forgive it. It can reveal hunger; it cannot feed it. That is why grace does not stop with conscience—it begins there and then moves toward the Cross.

Still, conscience matters because it is the meeting point between human responsibility and divine mercy. When a person who has never heard of Christ follows that inner law—choosing truth over deceit, compassion over cruelty, humility over pride—they are responding to Christ without yet knowing His name. The same Spirit who hovered over the waters hovers over every heart, pressing it toward the light. God judges not ignorance but refusal. Those who live by the truth they have are, in some mysterious way, already answering the call of the Word made flesh.

History is full of such hints. Socrates dying for the truth he could not name. Native peoples honouring the Creator they sensed but did not know. Mothers teaching their children to pray without knowing to whom. The Church does not dismiss these as pagan errors; it sees in them the fingerprints of prevenient grace. The Gospel, when it finally arrives, is not alien to them—it is the answer to a question they have been asking all along.

Yet conscience can also harden. The same law that can lead a person toward light can, if resisted, become the ground of judgment. When we know the good and refuse it, we do not merely break a rule; we break trust with the One who wrote that rule inside us. Jesus said, "The light has come into the world, and people loved darkness rather than light because their deeds were evil." That line explains both mercy and judgment. God does not condemn for ignorance; He condemns for refusal of grace. Light rejected becomes darkness chosen.

The genius of divine justice is that it meets each person where they stand. The scholar and the shepherd, the Christian and the one who has never seen a Bible—all are measured by the same truth, but each is judged by the grace they received and how they answered it. The bridge of salvation is wide enough for all, yet each must decide whether to step onto it. Conscience is the first plank under every foot.

For believers, this should not weaken mission; it should deepen humility. The Gospel we preach is not ours to boast about. It is the name of the grace that has already been chasing every heart. When a missionary crosses an ocean or a Christian shares faith with a friend, they are not bringing something new; they are revealing the face of the One those people have always half-known. Evangelisation is not invasion—it is recognition.

Grace written on the heart means that no human life is wasted. Even in places where the name of Christ is unknown, His Spirit works like groundwater under the desert. It breaks through in acts of mercy, in wonder at the stars, in the voice of conscience that refuses to die. One day every person will learn the name of the One who was guiding them all along, and they will see that every step toward truth was a step toward Him.

Grace always moves first. Long before we reach for God, He is reaching for us. The whole story of salvation turns on that truth. Creation itself began with it. God spoke into nothingness, and the void answered with light. That is what grace does—it speaks first. Every movement toward faith, repentance, or goodness is a reply to that first call.

Theologians call this *prevenient* grace—grace that goes before. It is the quiet work of God that prepares the ground before the seed of the Gospel is planted. It stirs questions in the mind, unease in the conscience, longing in the heart. It draws a person toward truth without forcing them. Wherever people begin to ask, *What is good?*

GRACE IN THE WORLD: HOW CHRIST REACHES THE UNREACHED

Who is God? Why am I here? prevenient grace is already at work. It is the invisible hand that turns the face toward the light before the light has a name.

Scripture is full of this pattern. Abraham did not seek out God; God called him. Moses was found in exile before he found his mission. Mary heard the angel before she could answer "yes." Peter was caught in a net of mercy before he ever preached a sermon. In each case, grace arrived first. The initiative is always God's. Human freedom is real, but it is response, not origin. We do not ignite faith; we consent to fire already burning.

This is why Christianity can hold hope for every person. Wherever the image of God remains, grace can reach. The Spirit moves through creation like wind—unseen, unpredictable, impossible to cage. Jesus used that image deliberately: "The wind blows where it wills; you hear its sound, but you do not know where it comes from or where it goes." The same wind that carried Him into the wilderness carries His whisper into every culture and age. Prevenient grace is that breath at work.

Sometimes it shows itself in restlessness. Augustine described it when he wrote, "You have made us for Yourself, O Lord, and our hearts are restless until they rest in You." The restlessness itself is grace. It is the ache of a soul being pulled home. No human desire —whether for beauty, justice, or love—exists apart from God's prior desire for us. Every longing for meaning is a hint of His pursuit. Even doubt can be grace in disguise: the mind protesting its hunger for truth.

Prevenient grace also explains why conversion often begins in fragments. A person might encounter kindness that feels undeserved, a beauty that leaves them silent, a sorrow that cracks their pride. In those moments, something larger presses in. Grace is close. It rarely announces itself; it simply makes escape impossible. C.S. Lewis called his own conversion being "surprised by joy." He thought he was chasing joy, but discovered joy had been chasing him. That is prevenient grace—God turning pursuit inside out.

This grace is universal but not automatic. It does not erase freedom; it awakens it. A person can cooperate with it or resist it. The same sunlight that softens wax hardens clay. The difference lies not in the sun but in the heart. Prevenient grace calls; saving grace completes. Every response of faith, every act of repentance, every cry for mercy begins because prevenient grace has already touched the will. To ignore it is to close the door on the only light that can guide us home.

For believers, understanding this should breed humility, not complacency. We were not clever enough to find God; He found us. Evangelisation is therefore not about conquest but about confirmation—recognising in others the grace that has already begun. Missionaries do not drag God into new places; they follow the traces of His footprints. Wherever compassion or truth or beauty glimmers, the Spirit has arrived before us. The task is to name what the heart already knows.

For those outside of Christianity, prevenient grace is the thread that ties them still to Christ. It is how the Logos—the eternal Word through whom all things were made—continues to speak inside His creation. When a person acts against injustice, when they forgive an enemy, when they kneel before mystery even without a name, that thread is pulling tight. Grace does not wait for permission. It moves through conscience, culture, and history, preparing every heart for the moment of encounter.

Yet prevenient grace is not the Gospel itself. It is its doorway. It awakens the question that only Christ can answer. The restlessness of the world, its endless search for peace, wealth, or pleasure, shows what happens when that question is ignored. The heart built for God tries to fill itself with substitutes and calls the ache freedom. But the ache remains until it finds its true object. That is why every genuine seeker, whatever they call themselves, is on the edge of revelation. Grace has led them there.

The wonder of this teaching is that it leaves no one beyond hope. God's initiative means no culture is abandoned, no life is wasted. The Spirit is always ahead of us, quietly preparing the soil of the world. Our task is to join the harvest, to speak the name of the One the world already senses. When we do, prevenient grace becomes saving grace; the question becomes answer; the search becomes homecoming.

If prevenient grace is the first movement of God toward every heart, judgment is the final measure of how each heart has responded. The question every person faces is not, "Did you know Christ by name?" but, "What did you do with the grace that found you?" Salvation and judgment are not arbitrary verdicts; they are the culmination of a conversation that has been going on between God and every soul since birth.

Scripture speaks about this with both gravity and hope. Jesus said, "The light has come into the world, but people loved darkness rather than light because their deeds were evil." That line is not a threat; it is a description of how reality works. When light shines, everything in its path is revealed. Some welcome it, some turn away, and in that turning the judgment already occurs. Hell, in Christian theology, is not primarily God's decision to reject the sinner; it is the sinner's decision to reject grace. The gates are locked from the inside.

This principle allows both justice and mercy to stand together. Each person will be judged by the truth they have received and how they answered it. Christ Himself says, "To whom much is given, much will be required." Those who have heard the Gospel bear the responsibility of that knowledge; those who have not will be judged by how they followed the grace written on their hearts. No one will face a standard they could not have known. Yet all will face the same Judge, because all grace is His.

The Church makes this distinction clear. Those who, through no fault of their own, never hear the Gospel are not condemned for ignorance; the same mercy that reached into death can reach them. Grace can find the child in a mountain village, the disabled person who cannot learn, the soul born into another faith that honestly seeks truth and good. Yet those who have received or could receive the Gospel and refuse it place themselves outside its healing. God does not reject them—they reject grace. Salvation is never earned, but neither is it forced. Love offered must still be accepted.

The early Church Fathers held this tension carefully. Justin Martyr wrote that "those who live by reason are Christians, even if they are called atheists," by which he meant that anyone who follows the Logos—the divine Word—follows Christ, whether or not they realise it. Irenaeus agreed, seeing in every act of righteousness outside the Church a sign of the Spirit's work. Still, neither man softened the edge of the Gospel. They insisted that grace unacknowledged is still grace offered, and that truth, once recognised, demands a decision. The same light that reveals also requires.

That is why the final judgment is described in Scripture not as a trial but as a revealing. Paul writes, "Each man's work will become manifest, for the Day will disclose it." Judgment is the unveiling of what is already true. Every hidden motive, every secret generosity, every neglected mercy comes into view. The books are not for God's information but for ours. Humanity finally sees itself in the full light of grace and chooses, once and for all, whether to stand in it or flee.

Christ is the measure of that choice because He is both truth and love. To encounter Him is to discover what our lives were made for. For some, that moment will be joy—the recognition of a Friend they have loved in fragments all their days. For others, it will be sorrow—the realisation that they spent their lives running from the only One who could make them whole. Heaven and hell are not rewards and punishments handed out at the end of the story; they are the continuation of the relationship we have already chosen. Grace extends itself infinitely; rejection hardens itself permanently.

The universality of Christ's mediation means that no one can escape that moment of truth. "Every knee shall bow, and every tongue confess that Jesus Christ is Lord," says Paul. Some will bow in adoration, some in regret, but all will see. The same sun melts wax and hardens clay. The same love that saves can also expose the refusal to be saved. In that sense, judgment is the final honesty between God and the soul.

For believers, this reality changes how we see the world. It removes both pride and despair. Pride, because salvation is never our achievement—it is always grace received. Despair, because no one is beyond reach until the last breath. The Cross still stands between humanity and its self-destruction, offering forgiveness to the thief, the cynic, and the indifferent alike. Until that final meeting, grace keeps working, keeps inviting, keeps interrupting the stories we think are finished.

That means Christians must speak truth plainly but never with contempt. When we warn of judgment, we are not predicting doom; we are describing the danger of refusing rescue. The call to repentance is not a threat but an invitation to live. The Gospel is severe only because the stakes are real. It tells us that every life ends in one of two directions—union with God or separation from Him—but it also tells us that God does everything short of violating our freedom to bring us home.

This understanding also gives meaning to suffering and delay. Sometimes we ask why God allows time to stretch on when evil seems to triumph. Peter answers, "The Lord is not slow to fulfil His promise… but is patient, not wishing that any should perish, but that all should reach repentance." Time itself is mercy. Every sunrise is God extending the invitation once more. Judgment will come, but only when grace has done everything it can.

In the end, every person will face the truth of Christ, and that truth will feel like love or like loss depending on how we have responded to it. The same fire that illuminates heaven burns in hell; the difference is whether we open or close our hearts to it. The Gospel is not a message of terror but of reality. God is love, and love respected must allow rejection. The tragedy of judgment is not that God stops loving the sinner but that the sinner stops wanting His love.

If every person is measured by the light they've been given, the Church's calling is to bring more light. Mission is not a human program; it is the continuation of Christ's own descent into the world. The same grace that moved Him from heaven to earth now moves His Body into every culture and language. Evangelisation is grace in motion.

From the beginning, believers understood this instinctively. The apostles scattered across the ancient world, not because they were restless travellers but because they had seen the bridge and could not keep quiet about it. Peter went north, Thomas east, Paul west; each carried the same story into different tongues. Wherever they went, they found that prevenient grace had been there first. Paul discovered a temple "to the unknown God" and used it to preach the known One. When the Gospel arrives, it doesn't erase the longings of a culture; it fulfils them. The missionary task is not to bulldoze but to translate—to show that the Word already spoken in creation has now spoken in flesh.

This is the paradox of Christian mission: it begins with the confession that God is already at work. We do not bring Christ to the world; we reveal Him in the world. He is the light that has been shining since the first day, even where it's not yet recognised. Still, recognition matters. A man can live by the warmth of a fire without knowing its source, but he cannot enter its full brightness until he steps into it. The Church calls every heart to that step.

GRACE IN THE WORLD: HOW CHRIST REACHES THE UNREACHED

Grace therefore has two movements—hidden and revealed. Hidden grace sustains the world; revealed grace saves it. Hidden grace keeps the universe breathing; revealed grace gives it purpose. When the Gospel is proclaimed, what was implicit becomes explicit, what was preparation becomes fulfilment. The difference between natural virtue and supernatural life is the difference between a seed and a tree. Both contain the same pattern, but only one bears fruit.

That is why the Church calls evangelisation a work of mercy. To proclaim Christ is to cooperate with the grace that already seeks every soul. The motive is never superiority but gratitude. Having been found, we help others be found. The Christian doesn't look down on the world; he looks out across it, knowing that grace is already in pursuit. The missionary simply names the unknown Friend.

This truth should also shape how Christians live in places where the Gospel is already known. We are not meant to hoard grace as a private possession but to become its instruments. Every act of justice, forgiveness, and compassion is a kind of sacrament—grace made visible through human hands. When the world sees mercy, it sees a reflection of the Mediator still at work. That's why indifference is the Church's most dangerous sin: it hides the light that others need to see.

The spread of grace also transforms how we see history. Empires rise and fall, ideologies clash, cultures shift, but underneath the noise a single story is unfolding—the slow redemption of creation. Christ's mediation doesn't end at Calvary; it continues through time, gathering fragments into wholeness. Every person who says yes to grace becomes another stone in the bridge. One day, when the last yes is spoken, that bridge will reach its farthest shore and the mission will be complete.

Until then, grace keeps working through ordinary means. The Church preaches, baptises, feeds, teaches, and forgives because those are the ways the life of the Mediator touches the world. The Spirit still blows where He wills—through saints, through sacraments, through simple acts of love that no one notices. Sometimes grace looks like thunder, sometimes like dew. The form changes; the source does not.

At the end of the age, the distinction between "reached" and "unreached" will vanish. Every person will stand before the same light that once descended into death. Then the full wisdom of God's plan will be clear: no one was overlooked, no cry unheard, no act of goodness wasted. Grace will have filled the world it created. Those who recognised it early will see how it carried them; those who met it late will see how long it had been searching. The Judge will be recognised as the same Saviour who once stooped to wash feet.

For now, we live in the middle of that story—between the harrowing and the harvest. The Church's task is simple: keep the bridge open, keep the lamps lit, keep naming the name that saves. Grace moves first, but it also moves through us. The only tragedy would be to stand still while it passes by.

The last word belongs to mercy. The Gospel begins with grace calling out of nothing, and it ends with grace filling everything. "Behold, I am making all things new." That is not wishful thinking; it is the promise written into the bones of the world. Christ will have the last word because He had the first. Every knee will bow, every tongue will confess, and every story will find its ending in the same sentence: Jesus Christ is Lord, and grace has reached the world.

7

The Good Pagan and the Unknown Christ

The Gospel insists that Jesus Christ is the only bridge between God and humanity. That claim has never grown less uncomfortable. From the first century until now, it has provoked the same uneasy question: *what about the good person who never knew Him?* Not as theory, but as faces. The child who dies before baptism. The tribesman who lives by honour in a jungle without churches. The mother who prays to a name she doesn't know. Are these lives simply written off?

The Church refuses to flatten either side of the tension. It will not soften Christ's words—"No one comes to the Father except through Me"—but it also will not deny the breadth of God's mercy. Salvation is never plural, yet grace is never stingy. The same Cross that stood on Calvary still casts its shadow, and its light, across every culture and century. The only bridge spans farther than our maps.

To speak honestly about this, we have to begin where God begins: with His desire that *all* be saved. Saint Paul's line is simple: "There is one God, and one Mediator between God and men, the man Christ Jesus, who gave Himself as a ransom for all." Those two words—*for all*—are the foundation of Catholic hope. Christ did not die for the converted; He died for the created. His atonement is sufficient for every soul that has ever drawn breath. Yet sufficiency is not the same as acceptance. Mercy offered can still be refused.

That distinction—between *reachable* and *reached*—is where most confusion lives. Some imagine that the moment we allow any possibility of salvation outside the visible Church, we have betrayed the Gospel. Others imagine that since God is merciful, belief is unnecessary. Both miss the centre. The Church's teaching holds the two truths in one hand:

1. All who are saved are saved *through Christ*.
2. Those who, *through no fault of their own,* do not know Him explicitly can still be touched by His grace.

That phrase, "through no fault of their own," matters. It is the moral hinge on which this whole discussion turns. Ignorance can be innocent or chosen. God alone knows which. The man born in the highlands who never hears a Gospel word is not the same as the man in a city who hears it, shrugs, and walks away. The first may be ignorant; the second, resistant. Heaven is open to ignorance that cannot be overcome; it is closed only to love that refuses the truth.

To make this concrete, imagine again the three lives that stand before us. The Afghan boy who prays to the one Creator and treats the poor kindly; the Amazonian girl who honours the Maker of the forest; the secular professor who sacrifices comfort for truth. None of them knows Christ by name, yet each has encountered the grace that proceeds from Him. The Church calls this *prevenient grace*—grace that moves first, that stirs the conscience before the Gospel is preached. It whispers through creation, through the moral law written on the heart, through the instinct for goodness that refuses to die. Where that grace is welcomed, the seed of faith already lives, even if the word "Jesus" has never been spoken.

This doesn't mean all religions are true. It means that truth, wherever it appears, already belongs to Christ. Justin Martyr called these glimmers the *seeds of the Word*. The Logos who became flesh is also the Logos who scattered reason and moral order through creation. When a pagan philosopher dies for truth, or a Muslim doctor tends the sick out of love for God, or a Buddhist monk practices compassion, these are not parallel paths to salvation—they are responses to the same divine initiative that will one day stand before them bearing wounds in His hands. The bridge has always been underneath their feet; they just haven't known its name.

Yet grace respects freedom. The same light that guides can be ignored. If the tribesman sacrifices his neighbour to appease a false god, if the scholar mocks what he half-believes because pride is easier than surrender, if any soul turns away from the good it *does* know—that turning is judgment begun. God never condemns for ignorance, only for refusal. Light rejected becomes darkness chosen.

That is why the Church preaches with urgency even while trusting in mercy. Christ's grace can save the unbaptised, but the Gospel gives them something better than uncertainty: clarity, sacraments, communion, hope named aloud. Mission exists not because God is limited, but because He wants His mercy known. The bridge doesn't need us to exist, but it asks us to point to it.

Every spark of goodness in the world, however faint, burns with borrowed flame from Christ. His light runs under every conscience like water beneath the ground. Mercy is wider than we think, but it still has a border—the edge where love ends because it is refused. The Gospel's last word is not leniency; it is love, wounded yet willing. The same mercy that can reach the unbaptised also judges the unrepentant. The Cross stands for both. It stretches its arms across every culture, and the hands that bless still bear scars.

The Church has never been confused about who saves. Salvation does not flow through ideas or rituals detached from their source; it flows from a Person. Jesus Christ is the only Saviour of the world. There is no second Redeemer waiting in the wings, no parallel covenant running beside His Cross. The question has never been *whether* salvation comes through Him, but *how far* His mercy can travel.

The Second Vatican Council faced that question directly in *Lumen Gentium* 16. It begins with a blunt truth: "Those who, through no fault of their own, do not know the Gospel of Christ or His Church, but who nevertheless seek God with a sincere heart and, moved by grace, strive by their deeds to do His will as known through the dictates of conscience, may achieve eternal salvation." The Church does not whisper this. It affirms that God's mercy is not caged by geography or literacy. His grace moves where missionaries cannot yet walk. But the same paragraph ends with an equal firmness: "Often men, deceived by the Evil One, have exchanged the truth of God for a lie... and serve the creature rather than the Creator." The text holds both realities in tension—hope and warning, mercy and truth.

The Catechism repeats it in its own rhythm: "Those who, through no fault of their own, do not know Christ or His Church, but who nevertheless seek God and, moved by grace, try to do His will as they know it through the dictates of conscience, may be saved" (CCC 847). The next sentence is sharper: "But very often, deceived by the Evil One, men have become vain in their reasonings... and have exchanged the truth of God for a lie" (CCC 848). Both lines together describe reality exactly as it is: the world is full of souls responding to light they can barely see, and full of souls who prefer the dark.

What the Church is *not* saying is that all religions are equally valid paths to God. That would be a betrayal of the Gospel and a denial of reason itself. Two contradictory truths cannot both be true. The same Scriptures that promise universal grace also warn of real loss: "Whoever believes and is baptised will be saved; whoever does not believe will be condemned." The meaning is plain. Christ's mercy is sufficient for everyone; yet those who know Him and reject Him choose separation. The Cross stands open to the world, but it must still be entered.

The word *may* in the Catechism matters. It keeps mercy from hardening into presumption. To say that those outside the Church *may* be saved is not to promise that they *will* be. It is a door left open, not a guarantee of arrival. The Church extends hope, not exemption. She never rewrites Christ's command, "Go and make disciples of all nations." Mission remains urgent precisely because salvation remains singular.

To say "outside the Church there is no salvation" was never a threat; it was a description of how grace works. The Church is not an institution competing for members; it is the visible Body of the one Mediator. Everything God does for the world passes through Christ, and everything Christ does for the world passes, in some mysterious way, through His Body. When grace reaches those who have never heard the Gospel, it does not bypass the Church—it flows outward from her. The saints, the sacraments, the prayers of the faithful, even the hidden holiness of the just—all of these are channels through which Christ's life moves into the world.

Yet the same teaching guards against false comfort. Ignorance does not sanctify sin; it only removes responsibility where responsibility is impossible. The man who never hears the name of Jesus may still be saved through Him; the man who hears and mocks, who sees and refuses, stands on different ground. Scripture never pretends the choice is unimportant. "Light has come into the world, and men loved darkness rather than light because their deeds were evil." The Gospel's warning is moral, not statistical. It reminds us that heaven is not reached by sincerity alone, but by grace received and obeyed.

This balance—mercy offered to all, truth binding on all—is what keeps the Church from both arrogance and sentimentality. The believer cannot boast: he was rescued, not recruited. The unbeliever cannot despair: he is sought, not forgotten. Christ's claim is universal not because He erases difference, but because He alone can reconcile every difference. The bridge between heaven and earth is wide enough for every nation, yet made of one wood.

The ordinary believer rarely reads council documents, but he lives their meaning every time he looks at the world with both realism and hope. To see a virtuous Muslim, a compassionate Buddhist, an honest atheist, should never produce contempt. Their goodness is borrowed light from the same sun. Yet it should never breed relativism either, as though truth were merely cultural. The sun is one. The Christian honours the glimmers because he knows the source.

That is why the saints could look at the pagans and still call them brothers without calling their gods true. Justin Martyr spoke of "seeds of the Word" scattered through the nations, not as excuses but as evidence that Christ was already at work beyond the Church's borders. Augustine saw divine fingerprints in every movement toward justice or beauty, even in those who had never read the Scriptures. Their insight was not modern tolerance; it was deeper realism. All truth, wherever found, belongs to the Truth made flesh.

So the Church's teaching stands as two pillars holding one bridge: mercy wider than we imagine, and Christ narrower than we wish. Between them lies the mystery of grace that works before belief, through conscience, and through creation—but always from the same Cross. When the Church says a person outside her visible walls *may* be saved, she is not lowering the standard; she is confessing the reach of her Lord. The "unknown Christ" is not a different saviour; He is the same Christ, unrecognised but still reigning.

The next step is to see how this plays out in history: how those seeds of truth appear in other cultures and why the Church calls them hints, not rivals, of revelation.

The ancient world was full of seekers who never saw a synagogue or heard a Gospel. Yet in the chaos of gods and philosophies, some still groped toward the truth. The early Christians recognised that these were not simply the "others" but the proof that the Word had been whispering long before He took flesh.

Justin Martyr, writing barely a century after the Crucifixion, coined a phrase that still echoes through theology: *logos spermatikos* — "the seed of the Word." He meant that Christ, the eternal Logos through whom all things were made, had sown fragments of His light into every human culture. Where a philosopher loves wisdom, a poet honours beauty, a ruler defends justice, there Christ is already at work in shadow. These were not rival revelations but reflections, broken shards of the same mirror.

Justin did not flatter the pagans; he named their limit. Their best insights reached upward but stopped at the clouds. Their virtue proved that the Word had touched them, but their altars proved that they did not yet know His name. "Those who live according to reason," he wrote, "are Christians, even though they are called atheists." He did not mean that Socrates secretly belonged to the Church; he meant that anyone who follows truth already walks a road that leads toward Christ, because truth is His native language.

That idea runs straight through Scripture. "The true Light," John wrote, "enlightens everyone who comes into the world." The Apostle didn't say every person understands the Light—only that no one is untouched by it. Creation itself is God's first sermon. The sky and the moral law both testify that the universe is not self-made. The psalmist could say, "The heavens declare the glory of God," because he knew that even the ignorant are surrounded by revelation. What we call nature is grace translated into matter.

The Fathers took this seriously. Clement of Alexandria described philosophy as a kind of "schoolmaster" preparing the Gentiles for the Gospel, just as the Law prepared Israel. Tertullian called the soul "naturally Christian"—not that it knows doctrine, but that it cannot stop longing for God. Augustine went further: "You have made us for Yourself, and our hearts are restless until they rest in You." Restlessness itself becomes evidence of grace; the ache is proof of design. The conscience of a virtuous pagan and the conversion of a Christian saint both begin in the same place—a heart stirred by the same God.

Yet the Fathers were not naïve. They knew that those seeds could rot as easily as sprout. They could be choked by idolatry, pride, or fear. The same impulse that builds a temple can also forge an idol. The same hunger for transcendence that leads a thinker to truth can lead another to the occult. The line between search and superstition is razor thin. That is why the Church honours the noble pagans but does not canonise their religions. The light in them is real, but it does not belong to them. The wheat and the weeds grow together until the harvest.

Socrates is often used as an example. He died for conscience, condemned for urging his students to love truth above convenience. His last words, thanking the gods for life, carry the gravity of a man who sensed a holiness larger than his imagination. The Church Fathers saw in him a kind of pre-Christian martyr—a witness to the Logos he could not name. When the Gospel finally reached Athens, it did not mock Socrates; it fulfilled him. The same courage that brought him to drink the hemlock now called new believers to drink the cup of Christ.

The same pattern can be traced across the world. Among the Stoics, reason was divine and virtue its imitation. In Chinese philosophy, order and harmony were seen as reflections of Heaven's law. In India, longing for release from suffering revealed the soul's hunger for redemption, even when it was misread as dissolution. In every culture, the Spirit left fingerprints. But the fingerprints are not the hand. The "unknown God" Paul preached in Athens was not another idol added to the shelf; He was the shelf's Maker come to knock it down.

This distinction is what keeps admiration from turning into syncretism. The Church honours what is true in other faiths because it already belongs to Christ, not because He belongs to them. Every moral truth, every noble impulse, every act of self-sacrifice outside the Church draws its energy from the same Cross. There are no "independent goods" in creation; only borrowed light. The more earnestly people follow that light, the closer they come to its source. When the Gospel arrives, they will recognise its voice not as new but as finally clear.

The missionary who steps onto foreign soil, then, does not bring God to the people; he reveals the God who has already been speaking in their language. The Gospel is translation, not invasion. "What you worship as unknown," said Paul, "this I proclaim to you." His words still name the Church's task. The Christian sees in every altar, every myth, every yearning, a signpost bent toward the same horizon. The Church does not steal the symbols of other cultures; it baptises them, washes away their falsehood, and keeps their truth.

When Christ entered the world, He did not destroy its questions; He answered them. The Cross is not an interruption in humanity's story; it is its centre. The wisdom of Greece, the longing of India, the justice of Israel, the discipline of Islam—all find their completion, not their cancellation, in Him. He is the Logos the philosophers guessed at, the fulfilment of the law the prophets proclaimed, the face of the mercy all humanity dimly hoped was real.

That is what the early Church meant by calling Him "the Desire of the nations." Every honest search for meaning was already a search for Him. Every act of justice was an echo of His law. Every story of sacrifice was a shadow of His Passion. The world's religions and philosophies were not empty noise; they were the overture. When the

Word became flesh, the music resolved.

This is why Christians can look at the best of other cultures with respect and still proclaim, without embarrassment, that their fulfilment lies in Christ alone. The seed of the Word was scattered everywhere, but the harvest belongs to one Lord. The sun shines on every land, but it rises only once.

The sun shines on every land, but it rises only once.

That rising is what divides history in two: before Christ and after. Not because human calendars changed, but because reality did. The Incarnation was not another episode in the religious story of mankind; it was the invasion of that story by its Author. Every philosophy and faith before Him was an echo waiting for a voice. Every sacrifice, every ritual washing, every longing for immortality was an instinctive gesture toward a redemption that only God Himself could accomplish. When He stepped into flesh, myth became memory. Eternity entered time and gave it direction.

That is why the Gospel cannot be relativised. It is not one window among many looking out on divine mystery. It is the view from inside God's house. The other religions contain rays of light; Christianity contains the Sun. To say this is not arrogance; it is gratitude. No human mind could have invented the scandal of the Cross—God dying at the hands of His creatures, love bleeding to atone for betrayal. The Gospel is true precisely because it is too strange to be our creation.

At the same time, Christ's coming does not erase the goodness that preceded Him; it redeems it. When He walked the roads of Galilee, He was not entering a moral vacuum. He was entering a world already heavy with prayers. He answered them all at once, not by founding a new religion but by fulfilling the purpose of every religion—to reunite man and God. That is why the Church calls Him not the destroyer of the law but its completion, not the rival of the prophets but their fulfilment. Every faith that seeks truth finds its terminus in Him. Every temple that ever lifted smoke to heaven was a shadow of the one altar where His blood would speak a better word.

Still, humanity is capable of turning even its longing into idolatry. That is the pattern Scripture repeats again and again. The same hunger that drives us toward God can drive us into distortion when pride rules the heart. Israel built a golden calf within sight of the mountain where God had spoken. Athens built statues of gods made in man's image, and modern culture builds idols of man remade as his own god. The instinct to worship never dies; it only changes direction. That is why revelation is not optional—it is rescue. Left to ourselves, we turn our prayers into mirrors.

The uniqueness of Christianity, then, lies not in the nobility of its followers but in the humility of its God. Every religion tells us to ascend; this one begins with God descending. Others prescribe enlightenment, escape, or moral perfection. Christ brings forgiveness, incarnation, and resurrection. In every other system, man climbs toward heaven; in this one, heaven stoops down and lifts man up. That movement—from God to us—is what makes Christianity not simply truer but *different in kind*. It is not humanity reaching divinity; it is divinity reaching humanity.

This is what Saint John meant when he wrote, "No one has ever seen God; the only Son, who is in the bosom of the Father, He has made Him known." The religions of the world had groped toward the unseen; in Jesus, the unseen became seeable. He did not come to nullify their search, but to finish it. Where the philosophers asked, "What is truth?" He answered, "I am." Where the mystics yearned for union with the divine, He offered communion with His Body and Blood. Where men feared the judgment of heaven, He took that judgment upon Himself. The Cross does not sit beside the altars of the world; it stands over them, explaining at last what sacrifice was for.

This revelation changes how the Church sees every people and culture. She does not regard the nations as pagans to be crushed but as brothers to be awakened. She enters their lands not to erase their histories but to interpret them. When Christianity came to Greece, it purified wisdom; to Rome, it sanctified law; to Africa, it gave voice to courage; to the Americas, it turned awe at creation into worship of the Creator. The Gospel does not erase what is human—it transfigures it. Grace builds on nature, it does not demolish it.

Yet the same Gospel that fulfils also divides. Christ said, "I came not to bring peace, but a sword," because His truth cuts between what is real and what only pretends to be. It honours every search for goodness while condemning every counterfeit of it. A religion may teach compassion and still be false if it denies the Lord of compassion. A philosophy may honour truth and still fall short if it rejects the Word who is Truth Himself. The measure of every creed is the Cross. Whatever cannot kneel before it cannot save.

This is why Christian mission has always been both tender and absolute. The first missionaries to foreign lands did not come as cultural revolutionaries but as witnesses. They studied languages, learned customs, honoured whatever was noble—but they also brought a flame that refused to mingle. They believed the tribes and temples they met were not devoid of God's voice; they were waiting for its fullness. When they preached Christ crucified, they were naming the unknown Friend who had been walking those forests and deserts since the beginning of time.

That conviction still stands. The Church recognises goodness wherever it exists, but she knows that goodness cannot finish what grace alone can. The moral beauty of other faiths is real, but it remains incomplete without redemption. Sin cannot be reasoned away; it must be forgiven. Death cannot be trained out of existence; it must be defeated. Only one man has done either. The crucified and risen Christ remains the line no religion can cross or replace.

In Him, God has already said everything He intends to say. Every later revelation that contradicts His divinity or denies His Cross is not addition but subtraction. When Islam calls Him prophet but not Son, when Hinduism absorbs Him into a thousand deities, when secularism remakes Him into a moral teacher—each keeps a fragment and loses the whole. There is no second Incarnation, no newer covenant. The revelation is complete because God Himself is the revelation.

The world keeps searching, but the answer will not change. Christ remains what every age most needs and least wants: a Saviour, not a suggestion. He confronts our pride and consoles our poverty in the same breath. The good pagan, the moral atheist, the honourable unbeliever—they are not beyond His reach, but neither are they beyond His demand. Grace may find them in a thousand ways, but the Cross is the only door through which they will finally pass.

At the end of time there will be no strangers to Christ. The last judgment will not be a courtroom of theological trivia but the unveiling of reality itself. Every person will see what his life was truly built upon, and every hidden movement of grace will stand in the open. For some, that revelation will be joy; for others, it will be terror. Yet the Judge will be the same Saviour who wept, bled, and waited for them. No one will face a stranger.

Scripture describes that moment in stark language. "Every knee shall bow, and every tongue confess that Jesus Christ is Lord." It does not say only the baptised will bow, but all. The question is not whether the confession will be made, but when and with what heart. Those who loved truth and mercy in this life will recognise the face behind every glimmer they followed. Those who worshipped self will see the same face and turn away in pain. Heaven and hell are not arbitrary destinations; they are the final form of a single truth—Christ embraced or Christ refused.

When the curtain is lifted, the good pagan will discover that his decency was not self-generated. Every act of compassion, every honest prayer, every refusal of evil was grace in disguise. The Afghan boy will see the hands that guided his conscience were pierced hands. The Amazon girl will recognise in the Creator she honoured the face of the Son through whom her forest was made. The sceptical scholar will realise that the truth he served so fiercely had a voice, and that it had been calling him by name. Each will know that salvation was never a negotiation between religions, but a rescue that had been underway since Calvary. The light they followed was not neutral; it was personal all along.

Yet others will meet that same light and tremble. They will see that they were not ignorant, only unwilling. They knew enough to choose but would not bend. The truth had brushed their lives—through a sermon half-heard, a kindness undeserved, a moment of conviction quickly buried—and they had pushed it aside. Hell begins with that push. God does not bar the door; the sinner bolts it. Divine justice is not vengeance but revelation: the unveiling of a will that has permanently preferred darkness.

That is what Scripture means by "the wrath of God." It is not the rage of an insulted deity but the settled sorrow of love refused. Wrath is what mercy looks like to those who hate it. When the river of grace reaches every shore, it divides—not because the water changes, but because the hearts that meet it do. One drinks and lives; another drowns rather than yield. The Cross casts both shadow and light.

This truth terrifies and comforts in equal measure. It means that no one is lost by accident, but it also means no one is saved by assumption. Each soul's eternal fate is its own answer to a single question: what did you do with the light that found you? That light may have come as Scripture or conscience, as beauty or suffering, as the sudden knowledge that there is good and it must be done. However it came, it was Christ seeking entry. Every encounter with truth was a knock at the door. To open was to begin salvation; to close was to begin hell.

The Church's insistence that "there is no salvation outside Christ" is therefore not a slogan of exclusion but of realism. There *is* no salvation outside Him because there *is* no life outside Him. He is the source of every breath and every virtue. Even those who never heard His name live, move, and have their being in Him. The difference between the saint and the sinner is not who was loved, but who allowed that love to make them new. When the end comes, that is what will be revealed: not categories, but consent.

This understanding frees us from both fear and pride. We do not need to calculate who is in and who is out. We need only live as people who have seen the light and therefore must not hide it. Every act of witness becomes an act of mercy, every word of truth a chance to make hidden grace visible. Mission is not an attempt to replace what others already have; it is the invitation to step fully into the light that has already touched them.

The saints understood this better than theologians often do. They looked on the world with compassion, not suspicion. Francis of Assisi could walk unarmed into the camp of the Sultan because he knew that Christ had already walked there first. Mother Teresa could love the dying Hindu with tenderness because she saw in every face the face of the Redeemer. Neither compromised the Gospel; both embodied it. They knew that proclaiming Christ is not an insult to other faiths but a homecoming for their deepest desires. The good they found in others was the footprint of grace leading to the same door.

So the mystery of the "unknown Christ" is not an escape clause from evangelisation; it is its foundation. We preach because He is already present. We call every heart by name because He has been whispering to it since birth. The task of the Church is to make explicit what creation and conscience have been hinting all along: that the world is not alone, that mercy has a name, that the truth they have half-known stands before them in flesh and glory.

When the last day comes and the light is no longer partial, every person will understand what their life has really been about. The Muslim who prayed in sincerity, the agnostic who loved truth more than comfort, the tribal elder who governed with justice—they will all see the same Lord, and in Him the reason for their goodness. Whether that moment becomes heaven or hell will depend on whether they rejoice in recognition or recoil in resentment. The difference will not lie in what they were given, but in how they answered.

Christ will not need to speak a sentence. His presence will judge and heal, divide and unite, simply by being what He is: the Truth. The eyes that burned with compassion in Galilee will burn again at the end, and the world will see that love itself is the measure. Mercy will be absolute, but so will freedom. The universe will end as it began—in His hands, open and pierced.

The heart of judgment is revelation. When Scripture says that Christ will return to "judge the living and the dead," it does not mean He will weigh good deeds against bad like a celestial accountant. It means the world will finally see itself in His light. Every hidden motive, every secret mercy, every ignored call will stand clear. What we called luck will appear as providence; what we called conscience will reveal itself as His whisper. Nothing will remain impersonal. The universe will be flooded with personality—one Face filling all space.

That revelation will have no neutral witnesses. The saints will cry out with recognition: *This is the One we loved, even when we barely understood Him.* The righteous of other faiths will realise that the God they sought by half-light was not a concept but this same Christ, the Word they knew without knowing. And the unrepentant will finally grasp what they have refused. The light they dreaded will show them the horror of their own self-chosen isolation. Love, resisted forever, becomes fire.

The Fathers of the Church used to speak of that moment not as a trial but as unveiling. Basil called it "the day of naked souls." Nothing added, nothing hidden—only what is true remaining. The line between heaven and hell will not be drawn by decree but by desire. Heaven is the soul saying *yes* to what it has always wanted; hell is the soul that keeps saying *no*. Both are eternal because truth and freedom are eternal. Even there, God will not cease to love, but love unwelcomed becomes torment.

This vision strips religion of pretence. It means that no ritual, no creed memorised by rote, can substitute for conversion of heart. It means also that no accident of birth can damn a soul that loves truth. The Afghan boy, the Amazon girl, the agnostic scholar—they stand before the same Lord as every baptised Christian. Their stories differ in light received, but not in the demand to respond. The Judge will ask no one, "Which label did you wear?" but "What did you do with the grace I gave you?" The Gospel is not about belonging to a club; it is about belonging to a Person.

The justice of this judgment is terrifying precisely because it is fair. Each soul will see how many times God came near—through conscience, through suffering, through the love of another person—and how often He was welcomed or ignored. We will know how patient He was, how relentless in mercy, how far He went to rescue us. No one will say, *You did not give me a chance*. We will see the chances as clearly as the stars, and we will know what we did with them.

For those who have lived within the Church, this knowledge will pierce deepest. To have received the sacraments, to have held the truth of the Gospel in our hands, is both privilege and peril. We will be judged not against the ignorance of the world but against the grace we possessed. "To whom much is given, much will be required." That sentence is not threat but measurement. Grace is gift, but every gift calls for fruit. The same Eucharist that saves can also condemn if received in indifference. Familiarity with holiness can dull awe, and dullness is the slow death of faith.

The pagan who dies reaching toward God and the Christian who dies yawning toward Him will not stand in the same light. The first may find surprise; the second, shame. But the judgment will be consistent. Both will face Christ's love as truth revealed. The difference lies only in their readiness to receive it. The final division of humanity will not be between Churchgoers and outsiders, but between those who let grace have its way and those who did not.

This is why the Church's mission is urgent. We are not collecting converts; we are rescuing realities. Every person you meet is already in conversation with God, whether they know it or not. Preaching, serving, forgiving—these are ways of helping them recognise the voice that has been calling their name since before they were born. Evangelisation does not begin the dialogue; it names the Speaker. To stay silent, then, is not tolerance but neglect. To preach is not arrogance but gratitude for having been found.

The judgment also reveals how deeply God has bound Himself to His creation. Christ will not judge from afar; He will judge from within our humanity. The eyes that meet ours will be human eyes. The heart that weighs our lives will be the same heart that was pierced. His divinity guarantees justice; His humanity guarantees mercy. He knows our temptations because He endured them, knows our wounds because He carries them still. The marks of the nails are the world's defence in court. The Judge bears the evidence of His own compassion.

This is what makes Christian hope invincible. However the final reckoning unfolds, it will be conducted by the One who refused to save Himself so that He could save us. The Cross has already judged sin, and the Resurrection has already opened paradise. The last judgment is the public reading of that verdict. What remains is our agreement with it. Grace has written "forgiven" across every name; we must decide whether to sign beneath it.

For the redeemed, that day will be the unveiling of joy long hidden. The saints will see how their smallest acts of love rippled through time. The poor who forgave the cruel will discover how their forgiveness saved others they never met. Mothers who prayed in silence will see what storms they calmed. Nothing good will be lost; everything will be gathered. Heaven will not be an escape from history but its harvest.

For the lost, the same light will reveal the opposite: the waste of gifts, the long resistance, the pride that mistook itself for freedom. God will not need to speak condemnation; He will simply show what is, and the soul will pronounce its own sentence. That is the horror of hell—not divine cruelty but divine honesty. To stand forever before Love and prefer oneself is torment enough. Grace pursued them all their lives; they ran until there was nowhere left to run.

The judgment of Christ, then, is not a contest of religions but the consummation of revelation. Every faith, every philosophy, every conscience will face the same light. The true and the false will be separated as easily as morning separates night. And when the separation is complete, creation will finally rest. The long ache of history—the confusion of good and evil, the quarrel of creeds—will end in one clear vision: "Jesus Christ is Lord, to the glory of God the Father."

When that confession fills the universe—every knee bent, every tongue proclaiming "Jesus Christ is Lord"—creation will at last know what it was for. The long search of the nations will be over. The scattered truths, the broken philosophies, the half-guessed hymns, will all converge into one chorus. The question that haunted every age—*Who is God, and does He care for us?*—will stand answered by a scarred face radiant with love.

For the saints, it will be homecoming. The child who trusted, the unbeliever who acted justly out of reverence for conscience, the sinner who repented in the last breath—all will see that their goodness was never their own invention. Every kindness was His mercy borrowing their hands; every moment of honesty was His light passing through their eyes. They will not be surprised by grace; they will recognise it. Heaven will feel like recognition—the sudden realisation that every glimpse of beauty or tenderness in this world was Christ calling them forward.

For others, that same revelation will feel like fire. The soul that spent a lifetime defending its self-sufficiency will find itself face to face with the One it claimed not to need. The unbelief that seemed intellectual will reveal itself as moral: a refusal to be loved on someone else's terms. Yet even then, Christ will not stop loving. The sorrow of the damned is not absence of love but its unendurable nearness. Hell is love misunderstood—mercy encountered by a heart that cannot yield.

All of this—the hope and the warning—is why the Church continues to preach. If the world were already saved by ignorance, mission would be vanity. If the world were beyond saving, mission would be cruelty. But since Christ's grace can reach everyone and yet demands to be accepted, mission is mercy. The Gospel is not a competition between religions; it is a rescue shouted across time. When the Church speaks the name of Jesus to those who have never heard it, she is not claiming privilege—she is repaying debt. "Woe to me," said Paul, "if I do not preach the Gospel."

The same tension that runs through this chapter—mercy and truth, breadth and boundary—must live in every Christian heart. To believe that Christ alone saves should never harden us; it should make us gentler. We are not gatekeepers of salvation; we are witnesses of the Saviour. Every encounter becomes sacred because every person we meet is already known by Him, already sought by His Spirit. The grocery clerk, the refugee, the atheist colleague, the devout Muslim neighbour—all are loved with a love that went to the Cross for them. To know this is to live differently: less afraid, less superior, more urgent, more merciful.

The Church has always walked this path of confident humility. She proclaims a single way because she believes in a single love, one strong enough to reach everyone. Her saints have gone to every corner of the earth not to prove others wrong but to set them free. When the Gospel took root among pagan peoples, it did not erase their songs; it gave them new words. When it entered hostile cultures, it did not fear their wisdom; it fulfilled it. Christ never asked His followers to despise the world—only to name its longing and direct it home.

To live this faith now, in a century drowning in noise and relativism, requires the same courage the apostles had. The world insists that truth divides; the Christian knows only lies do. The world calls exclusivity arrogance; the Christian calls it reality. The Gospel does not apologise for its absoluteness because it is the only thing absolute enough to save. The Cross is still foolishness to those who perish, but to those who are being saved it remains the power of God.

Yet even as we proclaim that, we hold hope for every soul. The Church dares to hope for the salvation of all precisely because she knows who died for all. She does not presume to know who is lost; she entrusts all to the mercy of Christ. She knows that the Judge is the same Friend who washed feet, the same Shepherd who left the ninety-nine to find the one. In the end, every person who enters heaven will do so by the same grace, the same wounds, the same name. There is no other.

When history ends, it will not be a closing of doors but an opening of eyes. The child who died unbaptised, the sage who sought truth among idols, the scientist who refused easy lies—they will see that the answer to every prayer, every ache, every question, was a man on a Cross and an empty tomb behind Him. The good pagan will find the God he had half-known; the Christian will see the depth of the mercy he had only begun to grasp. And together they will understand what the Church has always meant by its hardest saying: *Outside Christ there is no salvation,* because outside Christ there is no life.

The final word belongs not to exclusion but to invitation. Grace is vast enough for the world, but it still asks for consent. The hands once nailed open will never close. They remain stretched across every border, still waiting, still calling, still bleeding love into the dark. The mercy that began before creation will finish what it started. Every nation, every heart, every history will be gathered into one sentence of joy:

Jesus Christ is Lord, and grace has reached the world.

8

Why Be Christian? The Joy of Knowing the Truth

Grace can save, but truth sets free. That sentence is the key to understanding everything that follows. The last chapters have shown that God's mercy reaches beyond borders, that the hand of Christ can touch hearts that have never heard His name. Yet Christianity does not end at being *reachable* by grace. It begins where grace is *recognised*. The difference between surviving on hidden grace and living in revealed truth is the difference between breathing and singing.

There are people in this world who, by no fault of their own, have never known the name of Jesus—and yet, by His mercy, they are not forgotten. Grace can find them. But those who have heard the Gospel, who have seen the Cross lifted high, have been offered more than survival. They have been offered communion. Christianity is not God's backup plan; it is the full revelation of who He is. It doesn't merely save from death; it restores what death destroyed—relationship, worship, sonship.

To be Christian, then, is not just to be *rescued* but to *know the Rescuer*. Hidden grace can redeem a life, but only revealed grace can transform it into joy. Salvation through Christ is possible even when His name is unknown, but *salvation known and celebrated*—the conscious union of faith, sacrament, and love—is the purpose of revelation itself. God wants not anonymous worshippers but children who recognise their Father's voice.

This is why Christianity matters. It is not a cultural label or a moral system but a miracle of relationship. The living God has spoken, and His speech is a Person. All religions ask the same question: how can humanity find God? Christianity reverses it: how can God find humanity? And He has—through flesh, through the Church, through the Spirit that cries out in us, "Abba, Father."

Imagine two men adrift at sea. Both are starving. One survives by collecting rainwater from storms, just enough to keep alive. The other is lifted onto a ship, fed, and brought home. The first is sustained by grace; the second is transformed by it. The difference is not God's love but the fullness of its expression. Christianity is the ship—the visible, sacramental vessel of grace through which the Father gathers His children from every sea.

This is why the Church never apologises for claiming to possess the fullness of truth. That claim is not arrogance but responsibility. The truth is not ours to boast about; it is Christ's to be proclaimed. The Catholic Church does not hold the truth as an owner holds property; she holds it as a chalice holds wine—poured in to be poured out. Outside her walls, the same Spirit still works; within her, that work finds its form, its nourishment, its clarity.

Grace can whisper in conscience, but revelation speaks aloud. Grace can forgive, but the sacraments make forgiveness tangible. Grace can be glimpsed in nature, but truth steps forward and names itself: "I am the way, the truth, and the life." In Christianity, mystery becomes communion, and God's presence moves from the realm of intuition into that of encounter.

This is why the Church insists that explicit faith in Christ, when possible, is not optional. It is the normal, intended mode of salvation—the unveiling of the face behind the mercy that all creation dimly senses. To live and die without hearing His name may not damn a person; to hear it and shrug might. Ignorance can be innocent; indifference cannot. When God reveals Himself, love demands a response.

The saints understood this difference intuitively. Saint Paul could say, "Woe to me if I do not preach the Gospel," not because he doubted the wideness of God's mercy, but because he had seen its centre. To know Christ is to feel the weight of joy too great to hoard. When the Samaritan woman ran back to her village shouting, "Come see a man who told me everything I ever did," she was not recruiting members to a cause; she was introducing them to the One who knew her. That is what evangelisation truly is—love made audible.

Hidden grace is like moonlight; it reflects the sun without revealing its face. Christianity is sunrise. The same light, but unshadowed, warm, and direct. That is why the Church calls revelation a gift, not a threat. It is the difference between guessing that you are loved and hearing it said aloud by the Beloved Himself.

To be Christian, then, is to live in the unveiled heart of reality. The doctrines of faith—Trinity, Incarnation, Church, Sacraments—are not abstractions; they are descriptions of what love looks like when it becomes visible. The world's religions are humanity's search for God; Christianity is God's self-introduction.

The modern world often asks, "Why be Christian when God can save everyone?" The answer is that Christianity is not a ticket to heaven; it is heaven beginning now. To believe in Christ is to begin the transformation that will be perfected in eternity. It is to know the One who already knows you. To receive the sacraments is to taste divine life before death. The faith does not merely promise salvation after the grave—it plants resurrection in the present.

This is why the Church calls baptism a new birth, confession a second resurrection, the Eucharist the medicine of immortality. In them, God's hidden grace becomes visible grace, objective, certain, tangible. What conscience feels faintly, the Church gives fully. What nature suggests, revelation secures.

So yes—grace can save the unreached. But the Christian life is what happens when the unreached are reached. When the veil is torn, and the hidden hand becomes a pierced one. When mercy acquires a voice and a name, and the human soul can finally answer back. That is the joy of knowing the truth: not that we are right, but that we are known.

Every age invents new ways to say the same thing: "All religions teach the same truth." The words sound generous, but they melt on contact with reality. If all roads lead to God, then God contradicts Himself, because those roads diverge in every possible direction. One faith says the divine is personal; another, that it is an impersonal force. One says history ends in judgment; another, in absorption. One sees creation as good; another calls it illusion. To claim that all are equally true is to say truth no longer matters at all. Christianity stands in defiance of that polite despair. It dares to say that God has spoken once and for all, and that His Word has a name.

Christianity is not one light among many; it is the sunrise. The world's religions and philosophies are like lanterns lit in the dark—some brighter than others, all helpful, but all dependent on a sun they did not make. When that sun rises, the lanterns are no longer needed to see the path. That is what Christ's coming did to human history: it turned guesswork into knowledge, longing into relationship, shadows into faces. Truth ceased to be a rumour and became a person.

That person, Jesus Christ, is not simply a teacher of wisdom or a prophet of virtue. He is the Wisdom and the Virtue of God made flesh. The Church calls this the **fullness of revelation**—everything that can be known about God and humanity's destiny is contained in Him. The Letter to the Hebrews puts it bluntly: "In many and various ways God spoke to our ancestors by the prophets, but in these last days He has spoken to us by His Son." Not *about* His Son—*by* His Son. The message and the messenger are the same.

This is why the Church guards the deposit of faith with such care. It is not defending an opinion; it is preserving an encounter. To change or relativise what Christ revealed would be to rewrite His face. The Church's inflexibility is not pride but fidelity to a Person. That fidelity is what we call *Catholicity*: the universality of truth rooted in one concrete body.

The Second Vatican Council expressed this mystery with precision: "This Church, constituted and organised in the world as a society, subsists in the Catholic Church." That word *subsists* was chosen carefully. It means that the Church of Christ continues to exist fully, in substance and form, in the Catholic Church. Not partially, not symbolically—fully. Other Christian communities share elements of sanctification and truth, but the fullness of those elements—the complete structure willed by Christ—remains here: one faith, one baptism, one Eucharist, one apostolic line stretching from Peter to the present.

To say that is not triumphalism; it is description. The same God who became visible in flesh continues to be visible through His Church. The Incarnation did not end at the Ascension; it expanded. The Body of Christ on the Cross became the Body of Christ in history. To separate Jesus from His Church is to tear heaven from earth again. The Head and the Body live or die together.

That is why every major heresy has begun with a denial of Christ's humanity or His divinity—and why every modern heresy begins with a denial of His Church. To say "I believe in Christ, but not in organised religion" is to forget that Christ Himself organised one. He chose apostles, gave them authority, and built His Church upon a fisherman's confession: "You are the Christ, the Son of the living God." The faith is not a club we join; it is a kingdom we enter, and kingdoms are visible.

This visibility matters because Christianity is not an abstraction; it is an incarnation. It has form, sacraments, a hierarchy, a continuity of touch. The same Christ who healed with His hands still heals through the hands of His priests. The same Spirit who descended at Pentecost still breathes in the Church's liturgy. The same blood that flowed at Calvary still flows in the chalice. Without that visible, sacramental continuity, Christianity dissolves into sentiment.

Here lies the essential difference between Christianity and every other religion. Islam reveres a prophet but denies the Son; it knows command but not communion. Buddhism seeks peace but cannot promise resurrection. Hinduism hungers for divinity but loses the person within it. Secular humanism exalts reason but cannot explain love. Only Christianity unites the infinite and the finite without confusion or division—God becomes man without ceasing to be God, and man is lifted into God without ceasing to be man.

This is not poetry; it is metaphysics. The Incarnation is the centre of existence, the point where all opposites reconcile. Eternity enters time. Spirit enters matter. Heaven enters the womb of a woman. The same mystery continues in the Church, which is not a replacement for Christ but His continuation. Her unity, holiness, catholicity, and apostolicity are not slogans—they are the visible marks of the invisible God dwelling with His people.

To be Christian, then, is to stand in the place where truth has become tangible. To be Catholic is to live inside that truth as a home, not as a theory. The Church is not perfect because her members are holy, but because her Head is. She is the only institution on earth whose Founder still lives. And the reason she claims to be the fullness of truth is because she alone contains the fullness of Him.

The world has no shortage of moral teachers, mystics, or philosophers. What it lacks is the one thing it cannot invent: a Redeemer who is both Judge and Saviour, both Creator and creature, both God and man. That is why Christianity cannot be improved upon, only accepted or refused. The bridge cannot be rebuilt; it already stands.

To believe this is not arrogance but gratitude. It is to know that we did not build the truth; it built us. The same God who stooped to wash feet still stoops to enter the chalice. The same Word who created galaxies still waits on the altar under the appearance of bread. No other religion makes claims so scandalous, because no other God loves so personally.

That is why the Church calls herself not merely a teacher of truth but its custodian, its vessel, its voice. She is not the source of light, but she is the lamp that holds it. The Christian faith does not apologise for being exclusive, because love itself is exclusive—it binds one to one. Yet within that exclusivity lies the universality of invitation: all are welcome to the wedding feast, but only one Bridegroom waits at the altar.

Jesus did not come to found a philosophy, write a book, or begin a movement. He came to build a Church. That truth offends modern sensibilities because we have learned to separate spirituality from structure. We imagine that belief can be pure while the institution that carries it is optional. But Christ never offered Himself in fragments. He is Head and Body, Word and flesh, divine and human, invisible and visible. His Church shares that same paradox—spiritual and institutional, heavenly and earthly, sinful in her members yet sinless in her foundation.

The Gospels record one of the most shocking promises in all of history: "You are Peter, and on this rock I will build My Church, and the gates of hell shall not prevail against it." No prophet before Him had spoken this way. Moses gathered tribes; David ruled a kingdom; Muhammad built a community of followers. But Jesus said *My* Church. Not one of many, but one. And He bound that Church's future to a person—Peter—whose name He changed to signify a foundation. The Church is not an abstraction of like-minded believers; it is a structure willed by Christ, alive with His Spirit, enduring through time.

From that moment, ecclesiology and Christology became inseparable. To know Christ fully is to belong to His Body. The same Incarnation that united divine and human in one person continues to unite heaven and earth in one people. The Church is not a human invention that later claimed divine approval; she is the extension of the Incarnation through history. The Word became flesh once in Mary's womb and continues to take flesh in the sacraments, in the Eucharist, in the communion of saints.

This is what the early Christians understood instinctively. When Saul persecuted the Church, the risen Christ asked, "Why do you persecute Me?" Not *them*—*Me*. The distinction between Christ and His Church does not divide; it reveals identity. To attack one is to wound the other. The same logic runs through all Christian theology: what Christ possesses by nature, the Church shares by grace. He is the Light; she reflects it. He is the Bridegroom; she is His Bride. He is the Head; she is His Body.

The unity of that Body is not symbolic. It is sacramental, real, and visible. It has form: bishops, priests, and deacons descending from the apostles; one Eucharist on one altar; one baptism into one faith. Apostolic succession is not a bureaucratic chain of command—it is a lifeline of touch. Every priest at every altar stands in a line of hands stretching back to Christ Himself. That is why Catholicism insists that the Church is not merely a spiritual gathering but a living organism sustained by grace. Her continuity is the continuity of the Incarnation itself.

No other founder of religion ever claimed such permanence. Muhammad declared himself a prophet; Buddha, an enlightened teacher; Confucius, a moral guide. All spoke truth as they saw it, but none dared say, "Whoever eats My flesh and drinks My blood has eternal life." None promised to remain with His followers "until the end of the age." None gave authority to forgive sins, to bind and loose, to offer His own Body as food. Only one claimed that His followers would share His divinity: "He who eats Me will live because of Me."

That is why the Church calls herself not merely a community of believers but the Mystical Body of Christ. Her holiness is not her achievement; it is His presence. Her teaching is not a theory; it is His voice continuing through time. When the pope speaks in communion with the bishops, when a priest absolves a sinner, when the faithful gather for Eucharist, these are not human gestures aspiring to heaven; they are heaven reaching into earth.

This is the mystery of Catholicism: that the eternal Word still binds Himself to matter. That salvation passes through water, oil, bread, and hands. That grace has addresses, calendars, and names. The Incarnation did not end; it expanded. The God who took flesh continues to touch flesh, and the Church is the locus of that touch. She is not a barrier between God and man but the meeting point where divinity and humanity embrace.

To reject the Church, then, is not to reject a human authority but to resist Christ's chosen form of presence in the world. Every generation has tried to remake Christianity into a private spirituality divorced from institution, as though we could have Christ without His Body. But a disembodied Christ would not be human; and a disembodied Christianity would not be divine. The Church's visible unity, expressed through the Bishop of Rome, is not a medieval invention—it is the continuation of that rock upon which Christ promised permanence.

This does not mean that those outside the visible Catholic communion are lost. The Second Vatican Council affirms that elements of sanctification and truth exist beyond her visible boundaries. But those elements, wherever they appear, draw their power from her. A river can flow beyond its banks, but it still comes from the same spring. Every baptism, every genuine conversion, every act of divine charity outside the visible Church is still the work of Christ through His Body.

That is why the Catholic claim is not arrogance but coherence. The Church does not compete with Christ for attention; she manifests Him. To belong to her is to belong to Him in the fullest way possible on this side of heaven. To leave her is to risk cutting oneself from the vine that bears the fruit of eternal life. "Abide in Me," He said, "for apart from Me you can do nothing."

To be Catholic is to live within that abiding—not as an insider's privilege but as a calling to deeper holiness. The Church is not a museum of the saved but a hospital for sinners, the visible sign that Christ still walks the earth, healing through His wounds. Every Mass is the continuation of Calvary; every confession a new resurrection. The same voice that forgave Peter still speaks through the priest's words of absolution. The same Spirit that hovered over the Jordan still descends at every baptism.

So why be Christian? Because the alternative is to live outside the fullness of what God has given. The Church is not an optional addition to Christ; she is His heartbeat made audible. The Christian who knows this can no longer treat faith as a hobby or private opinion. He belongs to a Body that stretches from the upper room to eternity. The world may call that exclusivity; heaven calls it communion.

Christianity does not promise escape from the world; it promises transfiguration. The world's religions and philosophies offer many versions of release—escape from illusion, from suffering, from sin, from self. But Christianity alone promises participation: not an exit from creation, but its renewal; not the abandonment of flesh, but its glorification. Salvation is not flight—it is union.

Every doctrine of the Church, from the Trinity to the sacraments, converges on this single truth: God became man so that man might share in the life of God. The Fathers called this **theosis**, divinisation—not that we become gods by nature, but that we share God's nature by grace. The Word did not descend to erase humanity but to raise it. As Athanasius wrote, "He became what we are, that we might become what He is." The cross was not a legal transaction but a wedding: divinity and humanity joined forever in one flesh.

This is what makes Christian salvation unique. Islam offers obedience; Buddhism offers enlightenment; secularism offers self-improvement. Christianity offers union—the creature brought into communion with its Creator. We are not merely forgiven criminals; we are adopted children. Grace does not merely cancel guilt; it re-creates the soul. The Christian is not simply declared righteous; he is made righteous by the indwelling Spirit. That transformation is not metaphor but participation in the very life of the Trinity.

Think of salvation not as a verdict but as a transplant. Sin is the death of the soul—the heart cut off from its source of blood. Forgiveness reattaches what was severed; sanctifying grace makes it beat with divine life. "It is no longer I who live," wrote Paul, "but Christ who lives in me." That is not poetic exaggeration; it is the anatomy of redemption. The goal is not that we behave better, but that we *become* new.

This is why the sacraments stand at the centre of the Christian mystery. They are not symbols of an absent grace; they are the instruments through which Christ acts now. Baptism is more than a declaration—it is the death of the old Adam and the birth of the new. The Eucharist is more than remembrance—it is the same Body and Blood that hung on the cross, given again to unite us to His life. Confession is not self-therapy—it is the reapplication of the Cross, the cleansing that reopens the arteries of grace. Every sacrament is the continuation of the Incarnation, the bridge through which divine life crosses into human flesh.

The difference between moralism and salvation is right here. Moralism says, "Try harder." Salvation says, "Abide in Me." Moralism reforms behaviour; grace remakes being. Without Christ's life within, even our virtue turns to vanity. The pagan can speak of justice, courage, moderation—but only the Christian can become a living temple of the Holy Spirit. In him, morality becomes mysticism: every act of charity, every offering of patience, becomes participation in divine love.

This understanding saves Christianity from two extremes: legalism and sentimentality. Legalism treats salvation as a transaction between sinner and Judge; sentimentality treats it as the assurance of being loved without being changed. Both shrink the Cross. The truth is larger. God's mercy does not ignore sin; it transforms the sinner. Forgiveness is the doorway; holiness is the house. The God who justifies also sanctifies, because His goal is not pardon alone but communion.

To call salvation "union with God" is not exaggeration—it is Scripture. Jesus prayed, "That they may be one, Father, even as You and I are one." Peter wrote, "We are made partakers of the divine nature." Paul declared, "You are the Body of Christ." These are not metaphors; they are metaphysical realities. Grace is not a moral mood but a real share in God's own life. That is why mortal sin is so grave: it is not the breaking of a rule but the cutting of a lifeline.

And this is why Christianity demands the Church. You cannot share the life of the Head while severed from the Body. Salvation is personal but never private. The same Spirit who unites us to Christ unites us to one another. Every Mass is a communal act because heaven itself is communion—one Body, many members, one life flowing through all. The Church is not the crowd of the saved; she is the organism through which saving grace circulates.

This is also why evangelisation matters. To share the Gospel is to share life itself. The missionary is not recruiting but transfusing. Every soul joined to Christ expands the Body and strengthens the world's heartbeat. The Christian who keeps silent hoards oxygen in a world suffocating for it.

Salvation, then, is not escape but restoration—creation healed, humanity reborn, cosmos transfigured. The resurrection of Christ was not a private miracle; it was the first movement of a new creation. The world still groans, but it groans in labour, not in death. Each believer, united to Christ, becomes part of that renewal. "Behold, I make all things new" is not only prophecy; it is process.

Why be Christian? Because nowhere else is life so complete, forgiveness so creative, or love so personal. Every religion tells man to climb toward the light; Christianity reveals that the Light has descended to dwell in him. To be Christian is not to follow a moral code but to enter a new existence. In Christ, we become what humanity was meant to be: sons and daughters radiant with divine life.

Christianity is not a system of rituals; it is a relationship that uses ritual to stay alive. Every creed, every commandment, every sacrament exists to sustain that relationship. The heartbeat of Christian faith is not rule-keeping but communion—the living bond between the soul and the Person of Jesus Christ. Without that, the moral law becomes suffocating and the liturgy becomes theatre. With it, both become windows into eternity.

Faith is not mental agreement to doctrines, nor is it blind optimism. It is trust grounded in a Person who has proven Himself trustworthy through death and resurrection. The Christian creed begins with "I believe in God," not "I believe that God exists." The difference is intimacy. To believe *in* someone is to lean on them, to stake your life on their word. That is why Christian faith cannot be reduced to philosophy; it is a covenant. We do not merely assent to truths about God—we enter into His life.

This relationship is not imaginary. It is mediated through the sacraments because Christ does not love in abstraction. He touches us the way He touched lepers—through matter, through the ordinary, through things that can be broken and blessed. Baptism is His embrace; the Eucharist is His heart beating in ours. To receive communion is not symbolic participation in a distant God but real union with the living Christ. The same Jesus who walked the roads of Galilee now walks the roads of our veins.

Here lies the great paradox of Christianity: its realism. Every other religion keeps a safe distance between the divine and the human. The gods of Olympus demand offerings but never offer themselves. The Allah of Islam rules by decree but remains unapproachable. The gods of Hinduism and Buddhism dissolve individuality into the ocean of being. Only Christianity brings God so close that He can be consumed, loved, and betrayed. The Infinite takes bread into His hands and says, "This is My Body."

That sentence undoes all philosophy and all myth. The Creator who spoke galaxies into motion now speaks to a single soul, "Take and eat." Faith means trusting that voice, and love means answering it. Christianity does not begin with human longing; it begins with divine invitation. "You did not choose Me," Christ says, "but I chose you." To believe is to accept being chosen.

This is why Christianity cannot be reduced to moral improvement. The moral life is the fruit of faith, not its substitute. To live virtuously without Christ is possible; to live divinely without Him is not. The Christian life is participation in His own obedience to the Father—obedience animated by love, not fear. The commandments cease to be burdens because they become descriptions of the beloved's heart. When Jesus says, "If you love Me, keep My commandments," He is not demanding performance but offering intimacy. Morality becomes worship when it flows from communion.

Prayer, too, becomes something larger than request. It is not sending messages to a distant throne; it is breathing with the Spirit who dwells within. The Christian does not climb toward God in prayer; he turns inward to meet the One already present. "The kingdom of God is within you," Christ said—not meaning that divinity is native to man, but that the indwelling Spirit makes the soul His temple. When we pray, we echo the heartbeat of heaven already pulsing inside us.

This is why personal relationship with Christ is not Protestant invention but Catholic essence. The saints knew Him personally because they lived inside the life of the Church. The Eucharist was not for them a reminder but a meeting. When Francis of Assisi wept before the crucifix, he was not performing emotion; he was recognising a Friend who had loved him first. When Teresa of Ávila wrote of prayer as "conversation with the One who we know loves us," she spoke of something as real as the ground beneath her feet. The mystics are not exceptions—they are demonstrations of what the sacraments make possible.

Faith, then, is not opposed to experience; it deepens it. It is not the rejection of reason but its fulfilment. Reason can show that God exists; faith allows us to know Him. Reason can tell us He is good; faith lets us taste that goodness. "Taste and see that the Lord is good" is not metaphor but invitation. Christianity asks for the whole person—mind, heart, body, and soul—because salvation transforms the whole person.

This personal knowledge of Christ transforms how we see suffering. When other philosophies tell the sufferer to detach, endure, or forget, the Christian sees a Cross. The Cross is not a riddle to solve but a Presence to meet. In every pain, the believer recognises the same pattern: loss turned to love, wound turned to witness. "I have been crucified with Christ," said Paul. That is faith's boldest sentence. It is not self-pity; it is solidarity. The Christian does not escape suffering; he finds Christ within it, and therefore finds resurrection waiting on the other side.

To be Christian, then, is to live a love story that no other religion can tell. A love so real it became visible, so humble it became edible, so faithful it became permanent. Every Mass retells that story: the Bridegroom offering Himself to the Bride, heaven stooping to kiss the earth. Faith is our "yes" to that kiss. It is not an idea; it is consent to be loved by God and to love Him back.

That is why Christianity cannot be replaced by any philosophy or moral code. Those can make men decent; only Christ can make them divine. To know Him is to be drawn into His life, to think with His mind, to see with His eyes, to love with His heart. Every saint, from Peter the fisherman to Thérèse of Lisieux, proves the same miracle: grace makes ordinary people luminous. The Christian's final joy is not that he believes in God, but that God believes in him enough to dwell within him.

Faith is not mere intellectual agreement to a list of statements, nor is it sentimental optimism. It is trust grounded in a Person who has proven Himself trustworthy through death and resurrection. Yet that trust is inseparable from truth. To believe *in* Christ is also to believe *what* He taught and *whom* He established to preserve that teaching. The Christian creed begins with "I believe in God," but those words already carry the whole deposit of faith—the Trinity, the Incarnation, the Church, the sacraments. Faith is both personal and doctrinal, covenant and confession. We do not merely assent to ideas about God; we assent to the God who has revealed Himself and the truth He speaks through His Church.

The Christian life does not float in isolation; it breathes within a body. The same Christ who called individuals by name also gathered them into one communion. That communion is the Church—not an optional add-on to faith but its home. The Church is not merely an organisation of the saved; she is the organism through which salvation flows. To belong to her is to live within the bloodstream of grace.

From the beginning, Christians have understood this. In a world full of temples, gods, and private devotions, the followers of Jesus gathered around one altar, one table, one faith. Their unity was not political but sacramental. What joined them was not shared sentiment but shared life. "Because there is one bread," wrote Paul, "we who are many are one body." The Church is not a club of believers who happen to agree; she is the mystical Body of Christ, born from His wounded side and animated by His Spirit.

This is why the Fathers called her the Ark of Salvation. Just as Noah's ark carried creation through the flood, the Church carries humanity through the deluge of sin. Outside her, the waters still rage; within her, the new creation begins. Cyprian of Carthage put it without apology: "He cannot have God as Father who does not have the Church as Mother." The saying sounds severe only until you realise what it means. The Church is not the alternative to Christ; she is His continuation. The same life that flowed from His heart on Calvary still pulses through her sacraments.

Every sacrament is a plank in that Ark. Baptism opens the door, washing the soul into a new creation. Confirmation strengthens the timbers with the fire of the Spirit. The Eucharist feeds the travellers with divine life itself. Confession repairs the cracks when sin strikes. Anointing heals the wounded as they near the shore. Marriage and Holy Orders extend the mission, multiplying love across the generations. These are not mere ceremonies; they are the structure of redemption. Through them, the flood of grace carries the world toward its home.

The Church's claim to be the one Ark is not arrogance; it is fidelity to her Builder. God told Noah to construct the Ark according to precise dimensions, and salvation depended on entering it. Christ gave His Church similar precision: "Go and make disciples of all nations, baptising them in the name of the Father, and of the Son, and of the Holy Spirit." He did not leave humanity to invent its own vessels of rescue. He built one and sealed it with His blood.

This is what "no salvation outside the Church" truly means—not exclusion, but dependence. Grace can work beyond the visible Church, but it never works apart from her. When the Afghan child or the Amazonian hunter responds to prevenient grace, they are already being touched by the Spirit of Christ who animates His Body. They may not see the Ark on the horizon, but the current that carries them is hers. The Church's borders are visible, but her reach is invisible. Every soul saved, even in ignorance, is saved through her mediation, because there is only one Mediator, and He acts through His Bride.

The Catholic Church alone contains the fullness of that mediation. Other Christian communities share elements of sanctification and truth—Scripture, baptism, prayer—but these derive their power from the same source and are ordered toward reunion with the whole. The Council of Florence put it succinctly: all who are saved, whether before or after Christ, are saved through the Church's merits. The Ark has many decks and open windows, but only one keel.

This truth both humbles and emboldens the believer. It humbles, because to belong to the Church is pure gift; none of us built the Ark. It emboldens, because to live within her is to stand inside the visible plan of God for the world. Her continuity is proof that Christ keeps His promises. Empires rise and fall, languages change, scandals come and go, yet the same Body continues to preach, baptise, and forgive. She has endured not by power but by Presence. The Church's endurance is a miracle of the same kind as the Incarnation: God dwelling with men, fragile yet indestructible.

To step into the Church, then, is to enter a living story—the same story that began when Christ called fishermen from their nets and told them they would catch men instead. Every Mass, every sacrament, every humble parish is part of that same net. The fisherman's hands have aged, but the catch continues. The waters of baptism still shimmer with the Jordan's light; the bread broken at every altar is the same that fed the Twelve.

This is why the Church calls herself catholic—universal. Her unity is not conformity but communion. Every tongue, tribe, and culture can enter and find their humanity not erased but fulfilled. The Body of Christ is not uniformity; it is harmony—many members, one life. The same Spirit who hovered over the waters of creation now hovers over the baptismal font, bringing order out of chaos again and again.

Why be Christian? Because to be Christian is to live within that Body—to know where grace flows, to hear the voice of the Shepherd speaking through His Church, to eat the Bread of life rather than chase crumbs of intuition. The world offers spirituality without truth, mysticism without incarnation, sentiment without salvation. The Church offers the only thing that endures: the living Christ made present in Word and sacrament, history and flesh.

The Ark is not a symbol. It is afloat. The flood has not ceased. And the voice of the Builder still echoes over the storm: "Come to Me, all you who labour and are heavy laden, and I will give you rest." To be Christian is to answer that voice and to find, within the hull of the Church, not confinement but freedom—the freedom of those who know the destination of the voyage.

Truth, when known, becomes a fire. It refuses to stay still. That is why evangelisation is not arrogance but love in motion—the overflow of a heart that has met Christ and cannot bear for anyone to live without Him. The first Christians did not spread the Gospel because they were ambitious; they did it because they were astonished. They had seen a man die and rise again, and the knowledge burned in them like sunrise breaking over a darkened world.

Evangelisation begins not with strategy but with gratitude. The missionary impulse of the Church is simply thanksgiving that speaks. Those who have tasted the Bread of Life cannot watch others starve on philosophies and guesswork. To proclaim the Gospel is not to impose one culture on another; it is to bring light to eyes already aching for it. Saint Paul's cry, "Woe to me if I do not preach the Gospel," was not guilt—it was hunger. Love kept expanding until it became mission.

The world, however, hears such urgency as threat. It calls exclusivity intolerance and truth itself an act of aggression. Yet silence in the face of error is not humility—it is indifference dressed as kindness. A doctor who knows the cure but withholds it because he fears offence is not compassionate; he is cowardly. If Christ is who He said He is, then evangelisation is not optional. It is the moral obligation of love.

But love never coerces. Evangelisation is persuasion through beauty, witness, and mercy, not domination by argument. The Church does not conquer by force but by fidelity. The martyrs conquered by dying well; the saints by living beautifully. When Francis of Assisi rebuilt the Church, he used no weapons but joy. When Mother Teresa converted hearts in Calcutta, she preached without words. Truth, when lived, speaks for itself.

Every age of history has produced two kinds of Christians: those who hide and those who radiate. The first keep the faith private, tidy, and safe. The second let it shine through cracks of weakness, through words and actions that reveal Someone greater. The saints were not clever strategists; they were burning lamps. And lamps do not choose who may see their light.

To evangelise, then, is not to recruit but to reveal. The missionary does not carry Christ into foreign lands as though He were absent there; he unveils the Christ already present and waiting to be named. The Gospel, when preached, is not a new sound to human ears—it is the long-remembered echo of home. The prodigal does not learn that the Father exists; he discovers that the Father never stopped watching the road.

This understanding transforms the entire mission of the Church.

Evangelisation is not an exercise in superiority; it is the act of returning to others what was first given to us. The Christian does not speak *down* to the world; he speaks *out* of love for it. God so loved the world that He gave His only Son—how could we not give His name in return?

The false humility of our age says, "Let each follow his own path; all roads lead to God." But if every road led to God, Calvary would be meaningless. The Cross is proof that only one road could bridge heaven and earth, and that it had to be built from above. To tell others this truth is not domination; it is mercy. The Gospel's exclusivity is its inclusivity—it is one bridge wide enough for all.

Yet we must learn how to speak this truth well. Evangelisation without holiness becomes noise; truth without charity becomes a weapon. The Christian must resemble what he proclaims. "By this all men will know you are My disciples," said Jesus, "if you love one another." The world will not believe our message until it sees in us the miracle we describe: enemies forgiven, joy in suffering, purity without pride, compassion without compromise. The Church's credibility has never rested on power but on sanctity.

Every Christian vocation, whether hidden or public, participates in this mission. Parents evangelise when they raise children in the faith; workers evangelise when they serve with integrity; artists evangelise when they reveal beauty that hints at the divine. The missionary and the mother share one task—to make Christ visible in the world. The same Spirit that drove Paul across seas drives grace through kitchens and classrooms.

Evangelisation is the Church breathing out what she has breathed in at the altar. The Mass ends with a sending: *Ite, missa est*—"Go, you are sent." Every Eucharist becomes a launching point for love. The Body received becomes the Body extended. The Christian who leaves Mass should carry on his skin the fragrance of heaven. To withhold that fragrance from a world decaying in despair would be the greatest failure of charity imaginable.

To love souls is to desire their salvation. That is the motive behind every mission, the fuel of every martyr, the reason the Church still crosses oceans and languages to speak one name. Christianity cannot be content with hidden holiness; it must become visible mercy. The Church exists not to preserve herself but to pour herself out. She is most herself when she bleeds.

To be Christian, then, is to join that pouring out. Every believer is a missionary because every believer has been found. We are sent not because we are better, but because we have seen the better way. Evangelisation is simply grace returning to its source—the overflow of joy that refuses to die. When the truth is alive in you, silence feels like betrayal.

The joy of knowing the truth is that it cannot be contained. Like light through stained glass, it spills outward in colour and warmth. It asks nothing for itself; it wants only that others see. To speak the name of Jesus is not an intrusion into another's story—it is the revelation of how that story was meant to end. Every act of witness, however small, becomes a participation in the same divine generosity that created the world.

And so the Church keeps speaking, keeps loving, keeps going. She knows what the world forgets: that the truth is not a threat but a rescue. Every "yes" to Christ is a liberation; every soul converted is another wound of His love healed. Mission is not conquest—it is communion expanding. When love becomes complete, it must be shared, and the measure of its truth is its generosity.

That is why evangelisation will never cease. The Gospel is not a slogan to be retired once heard; it is life itself spreading like fire across creation. The Christian who keeps faith private betrays its nature. The Christian who shares it, even trembling, becomes part of the great current of grace that began when a stone rolled away and a voice said,

WHY BE CHRISTIAN? THE JOY OF KNOWING THE TRUTH

"Go and tell My brothers."

The end of the Christian story is not exhaustion but joy. The closer a soul draws to the truth, the lighter it becomes. Every conversion—whether sudden or slow—is a rediscovery of home. To be Christian is to awaken from half-knowledge into daylight, to realise that all the fragments of meaning we ever gathered were pieces of a single face. That face is Christ, and in recognising Him, we recognise everything else.

This joy is not naïve or shallow; it is hard-won. It rises from the certainty that evil has been defeated and that suffering itself can be redeemed. The world's philosophies offer serenity, detachment, or acceptance. Christianity offers resurrection. Joy is not the denial of pain but the transfiguration of it—the laughter that breaks through tears when you see the tomb is empty.

That joy is the natural state of a soul that knows the truth. The saints radiate it not because they are spared suffering but because they have found its meaning. They live in a reality where nothing is wasted—where even wounds become windows. Every Eucharist renews that reality: heaven and earth joined, the crucified and risen Lord giving Himself again. To live in that rhythm is to live already within eternity.

Christianity alone dares to claim that truth is not an idea but a person, and that the person loves you. To know that is to step into a freedom no philosophy can manufacture. The truths of science and ethics can inform, inspire, and restrain; only the Truth made flesh can forgive and transform. Once that forgiveness is known, it must be shared. Joy, like light, cannot exist in private.

To be Christian, then, is to know the truth and to be known by it. It is to discover that the universe is personal—that reason itself has a voice and that voice calls you by name. This is why the faith is not an opinion but revelation: it does not rise from below but descends from above. Humanity's search for God ends where God's search for humanity begins. The Cross is the meeting point of both searches.

This is what Jesus meant when He said, "You will know the truth, and the truth will set you free." Freedom in this sense is not autonomy; it is communion. The liberated soul is not the one that does whatever it wishes but the one that finally wills what is good. Sin fractures the will; grace heals it. The modern world worships freedom as choice; Christianity worships freedom as love rightly ordered. The more you know the truth, the freer you become, because the truth you know is a Person who never lies.

In that light, evangelisation becomes an act of joy, not duty. To share the Gospel is to share the treasure of reality itself—to tell the world that meaning is not a mirage and that love has a name. When the Church declares "outside Christ there is no salvation," she is not building walls; she is opening eyes. Her certainty is not cruelty; it is clarity. There is one Shepherd because there is one flock, one Mediator because there is one humanity.

The Church's exclusivity, rightly understood, is her universality. She is not a sect guarding a secret but a Bride offering a banquet. Every sacrament, every act of mercy, every whispered prayer in her liturgy is an invitation to the feast. Those who reject it are not punished for ignorance but for refusing joy. Heaven is not the reward of the virtuous but the home of the forgiven—and the door stands open.

This is why the Christian cannot apologise for believing that his faith is true. To know Christ is to know what all hearts are made for. Every philosophy is an attempt to say what the Gospel already declares: that love is stronger than death and that the meaning of life is communion with the God who made us. Every honest question finds its answer not in new data but in a new relationship. Christianity is not merely correct; it is complete.

When the Church speaks of the *fullness of truth*, she means that nothing essential to salvation lies outside Christ and His Body. The

Catholic faith is not one option among many; it is the horizon of all that is real. The Scriptures, the Fathers, the saints, and the sacraments are not relics of the past but living arteries of grace that carry divine life into the world. The Church does not merely point to the truth—she participates in it, as the moon participates in the sun. Her light is borrowed but full.

This joy of truth transforms the believer. It makes humility possible, because truth is received, not invented. It makes courage possible, because truth does not depend on approval. It makes love possible, because truth and love are the same God under different names. A Christian who knows this lives differently—without fear, without cynicism, without the need to disguise his hope.

To know the truth is to be drawn into the divine dance of knowing and being known. The Father sends, the Son reveals, the Spirit indwells; and in that triune life, the Church finds her song. Every doctrine of the faith, every mystery of the liturgy, every moral teaching of the Gospel exists to lead us into that communion. Theology is not a map; it is an invitation to step inside the story.

At the end of all things, when faith becomes sight, this will be the cry of every redeemed heart: not "I was right," but "I was loved." Truth will not gloat; it will embrace. The joy of knowing the truth is the joy of seeing the face that has been seeking us since the beginning—the same face that looked out from a manger, wept in Gethsemane, and shone at dawn outside the tomb.

And when every tongue confesses that Jesus Christ is Lord, it will not be submission born of defeat but adoration born of recognition. The Truth Himself will be standing before us, and the universe will finally sound in tune.

That is why we are Christian—because we have seen the dawn, and because the light is beautiful.

9

The Only Door, the Open Door

There is only one door between heaven and earth, and it swings on the hinges of a cross. Every human life, whether it knows it or not, is lived in relation to that door. Some spend their days trying to build others beside it, some walk toward it in trust, and some stand before it without the courage to enter. But the truth is unchanging: there is only one door, and it stands open. Its threshold is wood and blood. Its inscription reads: "I am the Door; whoever enters by Me will be saved."

These words have always offended the world. They still do. A generation that treats every path as equally valid cannot tolerate a door that closes behind falsehood. The modern spirit wants a God who blesses all conclusions, a saviour who does not insist on saving. But the Gospel does not apologise for its clarity. There is only one Mediator because there is only one humanity. There is only one Redeemer because there is only one wound. The problem is not plural; it is singular: sin, the rupture between Creator and creation. The answer must be singular too: Christ, the bridge built from both sides.

That is the paradox of Christianity—its claim not merely to truth, but to truth incarnate. Every religion contains reflections of the divine;

Christianity contains the divine Himself. The prophets spoke of God; Jesus speaks as God. The mystics reached toward the eternal; Jesus brings eternity within reach. The philosophers sought meaning; Jesus says, "I am the Truth." The founders of other faiths pointed beyond themselves; He points to Himself and says, "Follow Me."

To call Him "the only door" is not arrogance but description. The structure of reality allows for no rival. The Creator and the creature are separated by an infinite gap; no human effort can close it. Religion may build stairways, ethics may lay foundations, philosophy may sketch blueprints—but the gap remains. Only the God who became man could build from both sides at once. In Him, the divine and the human meet without confusion or division. That union, once accomplished, became the single doorway through which all grace enters the world and through which all creation must one day pass.

This is why the Church proclaims Christ's uniqueness without apology. She does not compare Him to other teachers; she confesses Him as the truth that makes comparison possible. To call Him one among many would be to mistake the sun for another candle. It would be to treat eternity as an option. The Cross stands as the axis of history because on it heaven and earth met and kissed. Every salvation—ancient or modern, conscious or hidden—flows from that point. There is no other source because there is no other Saviour.

Yet if there is only one door, it is open to all. The same blood that stained the wood made the hinges move outward. The exclusivity of Christ is not limitation but invitation. The Cross is not a locked gate; it is a doorway thrown wide by love that refused to die closed. The arms that stretched across the wood were not drawing lines of exclusion; they were forming an embrace. That is why the Church can say in one breath that there is no salvation outside Christ and that His mercy reaches even those who do not yet know His name. The door is one, but it is open to every nation.

Still, the world resists. The pluralist says, "Surely all paths lead to God." The exclusivist says, "Surely only a few are chosen." The Gospel answers both: there is one way, and it was made for everyone. Truth is not plural, but love is universal. God's mercy is wide enough to reach the farthest sinner, yet precise enough to pass only through Christ. Every religion that seeks goodness is, in its best moments, groping toward that same door. Every conscience that refuses evil is already hearing its hinges creak.

The story of salvation is not a competition between faiths but the unfolding of one divine plan in which all humanity is invited. The prophets prepared it, the apostles proclaimed it, the Church preserves it. The Cross stands at the centre as both compass and threshold. Its vertical beam points to the descent of God into time; its horizontal beam stretches outward, embracing the world. The intersection between them is the heart of Jesus—the point where divine mercy and human misery meet.

The believer who kneels before that Cross does not boast; he surrenders. He knows he did not discover truth but was found by it. The door of heaven was not unlocked by argument or effort but by grace. To be Christian is not to claim superiority; it is to admit helplessness and to walk through the only doorway love has built. The saints understand this best. They know the narrowness of the way, but they also know its wideness. The door looks small from the outside because pride cannot fit through, yet once inside it opens into a space larger than the universe.

The Cross is therefore both boundary and bridge—boundary because it marks the end of illusion, bridge because it joins heaven and earth. It refutes both extremes of modern thought: the cold exclusivism that limits God's mercy and the warm pluralism that dissolves His truth. The first makes the door narrower than Christ's love; the second makes it so wide that it ceases to exist. But the real Gospel stands between them. There is one door, but it is open; one truth, but offered freely; one Saviour, but for all.

Every soul in history will one day stand before that threshold. Kings and peasants, atheists and mystics, believers and sceptics alike—all will discover that the same door has been before them all along. Some will find it familiar, the doorway they already entered by faith; others will realise, too late, that every good impulse they followed was leading there. The tragedy of sin is not that the door is closed, but that so many refuse to walk through it.

The Cross, then, is not just the symbol of a religion; it is the shape of reality. It is how love operates—descending and embracing. The vertical beam says, "God came down"; the horizontal, "for everyone." The whole world hangs on that intersection, and through it passes every act of grace.

The Cross stands at the centre of the universe like a compass carved into stone—its vertical beam pointing from heaven to earth, its horizontal beam stretching from one end of humanity to the other. The vertical line is God's descent; the horizontal line is the world's embrace. Together they form the geometry of salvation.

Every false religion and every human philosophy tries to draw one line or the other, but never both. Mysticism, stripped of revelation, reaches upward without answer—a vertical yearning that never touches the ground. Humanism, stripped of transcendence, stretches outward in goodwill but cannot rise above itself. The Cross unites the two directions. It is the one point where divine descent and human solidarity meet and stay joined.

That intersection is the heart of Christianity. God's love does not float in abstraction; it enters history, touches flesh, and bleeds. On Calvary, the eternal Word stooped low enough to wash the dust from creation's feet. The upward line of humanity's longing met the downward line of divine mercy, and the world's axis turned. Religion was not abolished but fulfilled. All that humanity had sought—justice, purity, peace, forgiveness—found its centre in a single act of self-giving.

The Cross does not oppose mercy and justice; it reveals their identity. Justice demands that evil be answered; mercy demands that the sinner be spared. Only love can satisfy both. When the Son of God bore sin in His own body, justice was not denied—it was absorbed. Mercy was not a sentimental bypass of judgment but its transfiguration. The Judge took the place of the guilty, and the verdict was life.

That is why the Cross must remain the compass of all Christian thought. Lose the vertical beam and you are left with humanism without heaven—charity detached from holiness. Lose the horizontal beam and you are left with piety without compassion—worship detached from love. The two beams together form the full shape of the Gospel. The one who kneels before God must also stretch his arms to his neighbour, because the same blood runs through both.

This is also why exclusivism and pluralism both fail. Exclusivism imagines that Christ came only for a chosen few, reducing the Cross to a private rescue. Pluralism imagines that Christ is unnecessary, that all faiths are equally valid ladders to heaven. Both misunderstand the beams. Exclusivism saws the horizontal in half; pluralism erases the vertical entirely. The truth is the Cross whole—one Saviour for all, one way that welcomes all who will enter.

The Gospel does not say that only Christians are loved by God; it says that only Christ can save them. Love is universal; redemption is particular. The Father's mercy extends to every creature, but His mercy has a shape, and that shape is cruciform. The arms stretched wide on Calvary are not barriers but bridges. They reach farther than every border and culture, yet they remain anchored in one Person.

This vision dismantles pride on both sides. It humbles the believer who might boast in his privilege and warns the unbeliever who presumes on tolerance. It tells the first: you are saved by grace, not merit. It tells the second: grace is free but not cheap. The Cross excludes boasting and excuses in equal measure. It levels the ground beneath all feet.

The first Christians understood this better than we do. They lived surrounded by temples and idols, philosophies and cults, each claiming a way to the divine. Yet they did not apologise for preaching one Saviour. They saw in the resurrection not an opinion but an event. If Christ has risen, then truth is no longer plural. The gods have fallen silent; the unknown is known. The apostles faced death rather than pretend otherwise. Their exclusivity was not arrogance but allegiance to fact.

That allegiance remains the scandal of our age. Modern tolerance mistakes indifference for love. It refuses to discriminate between falsehood and truth, as though sincerity could substitute for reality. Yet love without truth is flattery, and truth without love is cruelty. Christianity holds them together at the Cross. The God who declared "No one comes to the Father but through Me" is the same who said, "Come to Me, all who labour." The same voice that warns also welcomes. The same door that is narrow is never locked.

At the Cross, every argument collapses. The proud discover their sin; the sinner discovers his worth. The philosopher discovers that wisdom bleeds; the sceptic discovers that love has scars. God's exclusivity and His universality meet in the same embrace. One Saviour for all humanity. One door, open to the world.

It is here, at this intersection, that the Church takes her form. She is built on the lines of the Cross—rooted in heaven, stretched toward earth. Her vertical beam is worship: the liturgy rising from altar to throne. Her horizontal beam is mission: hands reaching to the poor, the ignorant, the estranged. If she loses either, she ceases to be the Church. When she kneels before God without serving her neighbour, she becomes a shrine; when she serves her neighbour without kneeling before God, she becomes an Charity. Only when both movements coexist does she reveal her Lord.

The Cross is not only the means of our salvation; it is the map of our vocation. The Christian life is cruciform. Every act of obedience, every suffering endured, every mercy offered traces that shape again. The Church does not merely remember Calvary; she relives it. In her worship and her witness, in her saints and her martyrs, the same geometry repeats: vertical adoration, horizontal love. The door once opened remains open through her.

The Church exists because the Cross did not end with a tomb. The Crucified rose, and in rising, He left His own life beating within His followers. That life had to take visible form; love had to become structure. The same God who entered human flesh now enters human history, continuing His work through a body made of many members. That body is not a symbol; it is a continuation. The Church is the living extension of the embrace that began on Calvary—the horizontal beam stretching forward through time.

When Christ's arms opened on the Cross, they were reaching not only backward to Israel but forward to the world. Every century since has been the unfolding of that reach. Through apostles and martyrs, monks and missionaries, the wounded hands of Jesus have never stopped stretching outward. What the world calls "the spread of Christianity" is, in reality, the ongoing movement of divine mercy. The same life that bled in Jerusalem now circulates in every sacrament and every act of faith.

This is why the Church is not an optional addition to salvation but the place where salvation becomes tangible. She is the household of grace, the visible body through which Christ continues to teach, heal, forgive, and feed. The Church's holiness does not lie in her members' virtue but in her Founder's presence. Her priests are flawed, her history scarred, yet through her flows the same grace that once raised the dead.

The treasure is in earthen vessels, but it is still treasure.

To step into the Church, then, is to step into that embrace. Every liturgy replays the geometry of the Cross. The priest raises his hands in the same shape, the people respond, heaven and earth meet again, and the vertical and horizontal merge into worship. The Eucharist is not a reminder of the sacrifice but its continuation across the centuries—the same Body, the same Blood, offered now through time. When the words "This is My Body" are spoken, the door opens again, and the world is invited to enter.

The Church's mission, therefore, is not to improve the world by moral persuasion but to remake it by participation in that sacrifice. She does not preach self-help but self-giving. Her goal is not to make people nicer but to make them new. She stands as the place where humanity's wounds are gathered into Christ's and healed from within. Every baptism, every absolution, every Eucharist is a thread in that seamless garment of redemption.

Yet the Church's existence also exposes the limits of human pride. The same world that hung the Saviour now mocks His Body. It admires her art and despises her doctrine, borrows her ethics and rejects her authority. But the scorn that once nailed Jesus to wood will not close the door He left open. The Church does not need the world's permission to exist; she exists because love willed it. She does not ask to be liked; she asks to be believed.

Still, her posture toward the world is not defiance but invitation. The Church does not stand at the door as guard but as herald. "Come in," she says, "not because you are pure, but because you are loved." Her mission is to announce that the debt has been paid, that the door stands open, that every sinner has a home. Even when her own children fail, that announcement remains true. The holiness of the message is not nullified by the weakness of the messenger.

This is why the Church's identity is inseparable from her mission.

THE ONE WAY

She is not a museum of saints but a hospital for sinners. The same blood that bought her birth still flows through her veins. Her very failures prove the patience of her Lord: that He will not abandon the Body He died to create. The scandals of history reveal the endurance of grace—that after every fall, the Bride still rises, washed again in the water and the blood that flow from her Bridegroom's side.

For two thousand years, the Church has carried that invitation into every corner of the earth. She has preached to emperors and to outcasts, built cathedrals and cared for lepers, taught kings and baptised beggars. She has been persecuted, exiled, betrayed, yet she remains, because her endurance is not her own. The same Spirit that raised Jesus from the dead sustains her. The Cross planted in the soil of the world has not rotted; it has taken root.

To belong to that Church is to live inside the embrace of God extended through time. It is to know that one's faith is not solitary but communal, not private but cosmic. Every Mass joins heaven's worship; every act of mercy echoes eternity. The Christian who understands this no longer asks, "Why belong to the Church?" but "How could I live without her?" For outside her walls, the storm still rages, and inside, the ark still floats.

The Church is the open door's living threshold—the meeting point of mercy and mission, of heaven's descent and humanity's return. Her sacraments are the hinges on which the door swings, her saints the light shining through its cracks. To enter her is to enter Christ, and to leave her is to leave the only place where love has a body.

Every generation is tempted to believe it can build a new door. The illusion takes many forms—progress without repentance, spirituality without worship, love without truth. Humanity's pride whispers the same ancient lie: *you can reach heaven another way.* But every door built from below collapses. The materials are wrong. The hinges cannot bear the weight of eternity. Only the wood of the Cross can carry divine mercy into human life.

This is why Christianity must always be both universal and particular—universal in its reach, particular in its foundation. There is one Mediator for all people, but He mediates through one covenant, one sacrifice, one Church. God does not scatter a thousand competing doors across the landscape of history; He plants one open gate and calls every tribe and tongue to it. The Cross stands taller than every temple because it is not built by human hands.

The exclusivity of Christ is the inclusivity of grace. The very fact that there is *one* door means that *all* may enter. If salvation depended on birth, intelligence, or moral perfection, it would be the property of the few. But it depends on the blood of Christ, which was shed for all. The door is narrow because truth is singular; it is open because mercy is infinite.

This union of narrowness and openness is the paradox of divine love. It cannot contradict itself, yet it never ceases to welcome. It refuses falsehood, yet it embraces the false. The same God who says "no one comes to the Father but through Me" also says "come to Me, all who labour." The Cross speaks both sentences at once. The arms that stretch wide forbid every rival saviour yet invite every sinner.

That is why Christianity alone can reconcile humility with certainty. The believer confesses one truth not because he has earned it but because he has received it. There is no arrogance in holding a key you did not forge. The missionary's voice is not that of a conqueror but of a beggar who has found bread and must tell others where it is. To proclaim Christ as the only Saviour is not pride—it is gratitude.

Yet gratitude must be spoken. Silence in the face of error is not peace but complicity. If we truly believe that the Cross is the only bridge strong enough to bear the world, how could we watch others drown without shouting its name? The Church's mission exists because love cannot remain private. The truth that saves must be told, or it ceases to be love.

The Christian task, however, is not to shout others down but to raise them up. Evangelisation is persuasion through holiness—truth embodied in compassion. The world cannot be argued into faith; it must be invited by beauty and healed by mercy. The same God who conquered by crucifixion still conquers by love that suffers for the beloved. The Cross, not the sword, is the shape of victory.

When the Church forgets this, she loses her power. Whenever she trades humility for dominance or truth for comfort, the door she guards becomes harder to see. But even then, the door itself remains open, because it was built by nail-scarred hands, not by ours. The Church's failures cannot close what Christ has opened. Her holiness is borrowed; her endurance is grace. That is why she continues to preach despite her wounds. She is not the gatekeeper but the wounded Bride pointing to the gate.

The Cross remains the compass. The vertical beam reminds us who opened heaven; the horizontal beam reminds us whom it was opened for. Remove one, and the Gospel collapses into sentiment or severity. Keep both, and the Church stays true. The vertical demands repentance; the horizontal demands compassion. Together they form the shape of love made visible.

At that intersection, every human story finds its resolution. The sceptic who spent his life doubting discovers that reason itself points beyond the mind. The sinner who thought he was unworthy discovers a mercy deeper than his sin. The saint who spent a lifetime loving discovers that the love within him was never his own. The Cross gathers them all—philosopher and child, pagan and priest—beneath the same mercy.

This is the genius of Christianity: that it can say, with absolute conviction, "There is no other name by which we must be saved," and still stretch its arms to the ends of the earth. The door is one, yet it faces every direction. It welcomes the scholar in his study, the mother at her sink, the prisoner in his cell. It stands open at every hour, the same yesterday, today, and forever.

To look at that door is to see the mind of God revealed in wood and blood. The vertical tells us that heaven bends down; the horizontal, that love reaches out. The Cross is both judgment and invitation—condemnation of sin, salvation of sinners. It is the moment when divine justice and human rebellion collide, and instead of annihilation, the world receives redemption.

The Church carries that mystery into every age. Her doctrine is the vertical beam—truth descending from above; her charity is the horizontal—love spreading outward below. In her unity, both beams hold. When she teaches, she points upward; when she serves, she stretches outward. Together, these movements keep the door open and the compass true.

In a world obsessed with self-made gates—political, philosophical, spiritual—the Church remains the last reminder that salvation comes from the outside. The human heart is a locked room; only the Crucified holds the key.

The key is love that bleeds. Every other system offers ladders—steps of enlightenment, layers of knowledge, moral codes, meditations, rituals, and achievements. Christianity alone offers a door, because only Christianity begins with descent, not ascent. God comes down. The Incarnation is the event that ends religion as man's search for God and begins salvation as God's search for man.

Every creed, every philosophy, every moral effort apart from that descent ends where Babel did: confusion and collapse. The Cross is God's reply to Babel—one language of love, one Word spoken once for all. "I am the door," Christ says, "whoever enters by Me will be saved." It is the most inclusive exclusivity imaginable. The door is singular, yet it stands open to the whole world. It will not change shape to flatter culture, but neither will it close itself to sinners. It remains, nailed in place, wide enough for every nation, narrow enough for only truth to pass through.

To enter that door is not to join a sect or subscribe to an ideology; it is to step into the life of the Trinity. Through the Son we meet the Father; through the Spirit the Son lives within us. This is why the Church insists that salvation is not a transaction but communion. We are not saved *from* the world but *for* God. Redemption is not merely pardon—it is participation. Heaven is not a courtroom where the guilty are excused; it is a wedding where the bride becomes radiant with the glory of her beloved. The Christian faith is not a moral system that makes men slightly better but a divine operation that makes the dead live.

This reality is what gives the Church her identity. She is not one path among many, because she is not a path at all—she is the body of the One who *is* the Way. Her sacraments are not symbols of absent grace; they are conduits of the same power that shattered the tomb. Her doctrine is not speculation but revelation remembered. Her authority is not human control but the stewardship of divine truth. When she says "there is no salvation outside the Church," she does not boast in herself; she confesses that apart from Christ, there is no life. She points not to her members but to her Head.

To stand inside that truth is not narrowness—it is liberation. Relativism traps the soul in uncertainty; false tolerance erases meaning. But faith gives both boundaries and horizon. It tells us where home is and why the journey matters. The world fears dogma because it confuses certainty with pride, yet every act of love begins with certainty—certainty that the beloved exists, that life has meaning, that good and evil are real. Faith is that certainty raised to its highest form: not arrogance but allegiance.

In this light, exclusivity becomes the very grammar of love. A husband's vow excludes all others because his love includes one. Truth excludes falsehood because it includes reality. The Gospel's claim that Christ is the only door is the same kind of fidelity: divine love refusing to share its beloved with lies. The arms stretched on the Cross exclude nothing but unbelief itself.

That is why the Church cannot apologise for her claims. To proclaim "Jesus Christ is Lord" is not to insult the world but to invite it home. The Christian who hides that truth in the name of politeness withholds the very medicine that heals. Evangelisation, rightly understood, is not conquest but compassion—truth spoken with tears. The Church's confidence is not arrogance but gratitude that such a door exists at all.

Look again at Calvary. The world sees a failed revolution; faith sees the hinge of history. Between two thieves, under a sign written in three languages, stands the one Door for every nation. The vertical beam pierces heaven; the horizontal gathers earth. Blood and water flow from the wound—baptism and Eucharist—the entrance rites of the new creation. At the foot of that Cross stand Mary and John, the first image of the Church: the Mother and the beloved disciple receiving the mission to guard the doorway for all who will come after.

From that moment onward, every altar became a threshold, every saint a living invitation. The martyrs bore the shape of the door in their own bodies—broken, yet unbarred. The missionaries carried it to the ends of the earth, not as a theory but as a Presence that heals and transfigures. Wherever a Christian forgives, teaches, suffers, or loves, the hinges move again and the door opens a little wider.

To reject that door is to choose isolation. God will not force His way in; love must be entered freely. Hell, in the deepest sense, is the soul's final act of self-locking—the refusal to step through the very door that stands open. Heaven is not a prize but a Person, and that Person waits on the other side, still bearing wounds as proof that nothing else was strong enough to open the way.

So the Christian stands before the world not as a gatekeeper but as a witness, pointing to the doorway that death could not shut. He says, with the authority of grace, that there is one Saviour for all humanity—one bridge that spans every abyss, one light that darkness cannot overcome. The Church remains the keeper of that flame, not for her own sake but for the life of the world.

The Cross is the compass. The Church is the map. The Eucharist is the open door through which the world still walks into the life of God.

And when history ends—when every kingdom has fallen silent and every name has faded—the shape left standing will still be the same: the beams of a Cross forming the gates of heaven.

The arms stretched wide on Calvary are the open gates of paradise, and through them the world is invited to pass.

Epilogue

The story that began in Eden ends at an empty tomb. Between those two gardens lies every ache, rebellion, and hope of the human heart. We began with a question—why only one way to God?—and we finish with an answer written not in theory but in blood. The One Way is not a system; it is a Person. It is not a path we discover but a presence that discovers us. Jesus Christ is not one truth among many; He is Truth made flesh, the life that animates all who live, the way that carries home every soul that will be carried.

When Adam reached for the fruit, humanity reached for autonomy. We wanted to be as gods, yet ended dust. History since then has been the long search for the road back. Every temple, every philosophy, every prayer flung into the dark is humanity groping for what was lost: union with the Source of life. But no matter how high we built, our towers fell. The distance between creature and Creator cannot be climbed—it must be crossed.

That is why God Himself entered the story. The Incarnation was heaven bending down to touch the earth, divinity putting on mortality to heal it from within. In Bethlehem, the infinite took a heartbeat. In Nazareth, the hands that flung stars into space held wood and nails. In Jerusalem, those hands were pierced, and the gulf between God and man closed in a single act of love. The Cross is not just the symbol of salvation; it is the shape of reality made whole.

On that wood, justice and mercy met. The Judge took the sentence, the guilty received acquittal, and love proved itself stronger than law.

Humanity's debt was not waived but paid. Sin was not ignored but defeated. The wounds that sin tore in creation were not hidden; they were transfigured. The Resurrection is the Father's declaration that the work is finished—the bridge holds. Every path to God now passes through those scars.

From that moment, the world changed. The fabric of existence was rewoven around the risen body of Christ. Heaven was opened, not as an abstract hope but as a living fact. Death, once the terminus of every story, became the threshold of glory. The same humanity that fell in Adam was raised in Christ, carried into the heart of the Trinity. That is why there can only be one way: because there is only one human nature, and it has been healed only once.

To be Christian is not to claim ownership of this salvation but to bear witness to it. The Church exists because the miracle continues. Her sacraments are the touch of the Mediator still reaching through matter; her teachings are the voice of the Word still speaking in time. The same Spirit who raised Jesus from the dead now breathes through her, making the old creation new one soul at a time. The gates of hell will not prevail, not because the Church is clever, but because the Cross already stands on the other side of every gate.

This truth makes everything else fall into place. We can respect other religions, honour their search for good and beauty, recognise in them echoes of the divine voice—but we cannot pretend they save. They are reflections of the sun, not the sun itself. The difference between reflection and light is not arrogance; it is physics. Christ is not one beam of enlightenment; He is the source from which every real beam comes.

He alone restores communion between Creator and creation, because He alone shares both natures. Only one who is fully divine can restore what divinity gives; only one who is fully human can offer what humanity owes. Every other saviour fails on one side or the other—too human to redeem, too divine to die. In Jesus, the paradox resolves. Eternity entered time, and time was drawn into eternity.

This is the joy of the Christian confession: that the way back to God is not a maze but a man, and that man is also God. Faith in Him is not mental assent to doctrine but participation in divine life. The Creed is not a theory of God but a declaration of relationship—"I believe in God the Father Almighty" means I belong to the One who made me, redeemed me, and now calls me home.

Every tear of repentance, every Eucharist received, every act of mercy is a step across the bridge He built. The Church is not a fortress defending privilege; she is the living witness that the gate of heaven stands open. Her dogmas are not chains but coordinates; her sacraments not superstition but medicine. The world may call her narrow; she calls the world home.

The exclusivity of Christ is therefore the generosity of God. Because there is one way, no one need be lost; because there is one Saviour, no one need despair. The narrow path is not hard because it is cruel but because love itself is particular. A husband's vow excludes all others precisely because it includes one beloved. Truth excludes falsehood because it includes reality. So too the Gospel excludes every rival not from pride but from fidelity.

The one way is open, but it is not easy. It requires surrender—trust in a Person rather than in progress, repentance instead of reinvention. To enter the door of Christ is to leave behind self-sufficiency and pride, to admit that we are not gods but creatures, not masters but children. That humility is the gate to glory.

The arms that stretched wide on Calvary have never closed. They remain open now, as real as when they first broke the hold of death. The same mercy that called to the thief still calls to the world: *Today you will be with Me in paradise.*

The question that began this journey was simple, even childlike: why only one way? It has been answered not by argument but by encounter. There is one way because there is one God and one humanity, one wound and one cure, one Cross and one empty tomb. The paradox of particularity turns out to be the secret of universality. The Way is one, but it is wide enough for the world.

The invitation is eternal. Every sunrise preaches it, every Eucharist renews it, every act of forgiveness whispers it: the door is open. The living God has made Himself accessible not to the strong but to the willing. The highest mountain of heaven now stands at ground level.

The end of all theology is not comprehension but communion. Words fall silent where love begins. When all the debates are done, the truth remains in a single name—Jesus—and in a single act—trust. The soul that kneels before the Cross learns more in a minute than all philosophers have taught in millennia. Salvation is not an equation to solve but a Person to know.

One day, every human life will stand before that Person. Every creed will meet its Author; every conscience will face its Maker. The same eyes that wept over Jerusalem will look upon the world once more. For some, that gaze will be joy; for others, unbearable honesty. But no one will be able to say they were forgotten. Grace has been hunting them all along. The Shepherd who left the ninety-nine has never stopped searching for the one.

He will not ask whether we found a religion; He will ask whether we found Him. Not whether we defended truth online, but whether we lived it in love. Not whether we called ourselves Christian, but whether we followed the Christ. The Gospel is both invitation and examination: *What did you do with the grace that found you?*

At the end of this road, the answer every heart must give will echo the book's beginning. There is only one way to the Father, and that way is not a ladder but a Lamb. "Behold the Lamb of God, who takes away the sin of the world." Those words have never changed. The one sacrifice still stands; the one Mediator still reigns; the one Church still carries His light.

This is the joy of knowing the truth: that the truth is not an idea but a Person who cannot lie and will not leave. To be Christian is to be known by name, forgiven in blood, and kept in love. It is to walk the only road that leads not to improvement but to resurrection.

One day the journey will end in vision. Faith will become sight. The bridge will no longer be needed because we will stand on the far shore. The Father's house will be full, its doors never shut. Every redeemed voice will join the same confession: *Worthy is the Lamb who was slain, for by His blood He ransomed men for God from every tribe and tongue and nation.*

Until that day, the Church walks on—still proclaiming one Gospel in a thousand languages, still holding one chalice for a thousand thirsts, still pointing to one Cross for a thousand wounds. She is mocked, misunderstood, divided in herself, yet she endures because her foundation is not her strength but her Saviour.

The world will keep offering alternatives—new prophets, new philosophies, new promises—but the human heart knows better. It knows that only love strong enough to die is strong enough to save. And that love has a face.

The first Christians summed it up in three words that outlasted every empire: *Jesus is Lord.* That confession remains the hinge of history and the hope of the world. Everything true in human longing, everything good in human striving, everything beautiful in creation finds its fulfilment in Him.

There is, and always will be, only one way to the Father. Yet that one way opens into an infinite horizon. The door of heaven is not narrow to keep people out; it is narrow because it is truth, and truth cannot multiply itself. The Way is a Person—Jesus Christ, Son of the living God—and to walk that Way is not to nod at a name but to live His life.

THE ONE WAY

To call Him Lord is to follow Him; to believe in Him is to obey Him. Faith without repentance is presumption; love without conversion is sentiment. The Cross does not save us from the need to change—it gives us the power to change. Every soul that enters the open gate must do so carrying the same marks as its Master: humility, obedience, and love that endures unto death.

The one Way is not a slogan but a sacrament. It leads through the waters of baptism, through the altar of the Eucharist, through the narrow path of daily fidelity. The Church is not an optional guide for those already saved; she is the living Body of the Saviour through whom salvation is given. To belong to Christ is to belong to His Church, to eat His flesh, to live His commandments, and to die His death in order to share His resurrection.

That is why the call of the Gospel can never end at mere recognition. The bridge must be crossed; the covenant must be kept. Grace opens the door, but holiness walks through it. Heaven is not reached by sentiment but by sanctification—by a soul transformed by divine life. The arms stretched wide on Calvary are the open gates of heaven, but only those who take up their own cross will pass through them.

This is the answer, final and full: there is only one way to God because there is only one God who has become man, one Mediator who has conquered death, one Church built on His blood, and one life offered for the world.

The door stands open. The call remains. Not all will enter, but all are invited.

And the invitation still sounds in every age:
Come, follow Me.

Afterword

There comes a moment when words must yield to wonder.

The arguments have been made, the logic traced, the history told. Yet Christianity is not a philosophy to master but a Person to meet. The One Way is not a map—it is a man who still speaks, still walks, still calls us by name.

For two thousand years, that call has crossed every border and language. It has reached kings and beggars, scholars and shepherds, the broken and the proud. It has found its way into prisons and palaces, into the quiet of bedrooms and the chaos of battlefields. The same voice that said, *"Follow me,"* still echoes through time. And every human heart must, in the end, answer it.

Throughout this book, we have followed the logic of that voice. We have seen why no religion, however noble, can heal what sin destroyed; why no human striving can bridge the chasm between the Holy and the fallen; why truth cannot be plural, because God cannot contradict Himself. We have traced the astonishing claim that in Jesus Christ, the Infinite entered the finite—not as symbol or myth, but as history.

But there remains one step that no proof can take for you: belief. Not belief as intellectual assent, but as trust—a surrender of the will to the One who has already surrendered everything for you.

That is the true end of this journey. It does not finish at the page, but at the threshold of encounter.

The world will continue to whisper that there are many ways. It will urge you to blend a little of everything—to take the teachings of Jesus but leave the exclusivity, to admire His ethics but deny His divinity. It will say that all paths lead upward, that sincerity is salvation, that feeling is faith. It will tell you that to claim one truth is to insult another, that love requires relativism.

But the love revealed on the Cross is not sentimental—it is surgical. It cuts through illusion to heal reality itself. The One who hung there did not die for tolerance; He died for truth, and the truth was love.

This is why the Cross remains offensive to the modern mind. It humbles both the proud believer and the self-assured skeptic. It declares that we cannot save ourselves—not through ritual, morality, enlightenment, or progress. It reveals that all our ladders fall short, all our towers crumble, and all our light is borrowed. Yet in the same breath, it announces something even more shocking: that God Himself has come down the ladder to carry us home.

Every religion in history testifies to humanity reaching for God. Christianity alone declares that God reached for humanity. The difference is everything. It is the difference between hope and despair, grace and effort, life and death.

If you are reading these words with uncertainty, that is all right. Doubt is not the opposite of faith; indifference is. The path of faith begins not with perfect certainty but with a single step toward the light you already see. Faith is not achieved by argument but awakened by encounter. Christ does not demand that you first understand everything; He asks that you trust Him enough to follow.

You do not need to ascend to find Him. You do not need to clean yourself first. The gospel is not "find God"; it is "God has found you." Wherever you are, however far you have wandered, you are already within the reach of His mercy.

Perhaps, like the paralytic, you long to hear those words: *"Your sins are forgiven."*

Perhaps you have spent years trying to prove your worth—to others, to yourself, even to God. The One Way begins where self-salvation ends. Grace is the hand that meets you when you finally stop reaching upward and let yourself be lifted.

I wrote this book not merely to argue that Christianity is true, but to remind us why it matters that it is. If Jesus is who He claimed to be—if the Creator really walked among His creation—then everything changes. The Cross is not one story among many; it is the axis of all history. The empty tomb is not metaphor but milestone, the moment death itself was unmade. To believe this is not arrogance—it is alignment with reality.

And reality, at its deepest core, is not a force or principle but love. Love created the world, love entered it, love bled for it. That love has a face and a name: Jesus Christ.

Every age must decide what to do with Him. The crowds in Galilee asked, *"Who is this man who forgives sins?"* Pilate asked, *"What is truth?"* The question now comes to us. If Jesus truly is the Way, the Truth, and the Life, then neutrality is impossible. We are either moving toward Him or away from Him.

The narrow way is not narrow because God is small—it is narrow because truth is one. The way of Christ is open to all, but it is still only one road. It leads not to restriction, but to freedom; not to moralism, but to mercy; not to self-improvement, but to transformation.

At the end of the day, every heart must decide what it believes about a single claim: that God became man, died for our sins, and rose again. Either that claim is the greatest truth ever told, or the greatest lie ever spoken. There is no middle.

If you sense that it is true—if something in you stirs at the mention of His name—then the invitation is already before you. Not from me, but from Him.

Follow me.

The road may be narrow, but it is not lonely. It has been walked by saints and sinners, by the fearful and the brave, by those who doubted yet still followed. It ends where it began—in the heart of God.

The search for truth was never meant to end in an idea, but in a face.

Look to that face.

There is no other way home.

About the Author

Matthew Sardon is a Catholic author from Melbourne, Australia, whose work is shaped by the depth and breadth of the Church's intellectual and spiritual tradition. Formed through extensive theological study within the University of Divinity and nourished by years immersed in both the Roman and Byzantine rites, he brings to his writing a unified Catholic vision rooted in Scripture, illuminated by the Fathers, and sustained by the Church's liturgical life.

His research and writing centre on biblical theology, patristic anthropology, and the mystery of theosis—how divine grace heals, elevates, and transfigures the human person. He is committed to making the Church's ancient wisdom accessible to the contemporary world, offering clarity and strength where many experience confusion and fragmentation.

Matthew is actively engaged in Catholic ministry, contributing to teaching, catechesis, adult formation, and parish mission. His work as a speaker and presenter reflects the same passion found in his writing: to awaken faith, deepen understanding, and help others encounter the transforming love of God.

You can connect with me on:
- https://matthewsardon.com

www.ingramcontent.com/pod-product-compliance
Lightning Source LLC
Chambersburg PA
CBHW060103230426
43661CB00033B/1407/J